PROPHETIC BALLOON MODELLING

To Moira

Thanks for the interview!

Love + blessings

John

X

PROPHETIC BALLOON MODELLING

Foolish Reflections on Work, Rest and Play

John Guest

eagle

Guildford, Surrey

British Library Cataloguing in Publication Data. A catalogue record for this book is available from the British Library.

Published by Eagle, an imprint of Inter Publishing Service (IPS) Ltd, PO Box 530, Guildford, Surrey GU2 5FH.

Typeset by Eagle
Printed by Cox & Wyman
ISBN No: 0 86347 362 8

CONTENTS

Foreword   7
Introduction   9
How to Make a Balloon Model   15

WORK: What We Have to Do
  1.   First Puff: Have to, Like to, Need to   21
  2.   Second Puff: As Soon as the Rush is Over   33
  3.   Third Puff: To Be or not to Be?   49
  4.   Fourth Puff: Radiators and Drains   57
  5.   Fifth Puff: Improving Your Aim   71
  6.   Sixth Puff: Passion Restored
       and Work Redeemed   79

PLAY: What We Like to Do
  7.   First Twist: Send in the Clowns   95
  8.   Second Twist: Circles   107
  9.   Third Twist: Once Upon a Time   119
 10.   Fourth Twist: The Games We Play   127
 11.   Fifth Twist: Laughter – The Best Medicine   139
 12.   Sixth Twist: Playgrounds   149

REST: What We Need to Do
 13.   First Breath: Holidays   165
 14.   Second Breath: Keeping the Sabbath   173
 15.   Third Breath: Lessons from the Exodus   181
 16.   Fourth Breath: Lessons from Joshua   189
 17.   Fifth Breath: Waiting in Weakness   201
 18.   Sixth Breath: Do Less – Be More   213

Conclusion: Prophetic Balloon Modelling   221
Notes   233
Further Reading   236
Resources   238

To Kim
Every perfectionist needs a life project.
Thanks for making me yours.

Foreword

My old mate John and I go back a long way, so I was thrilled when he asked me to write the foreword to his first book. However, all I can say is that it's the biggest load of rubbish I've every read!

Take that subtitle, for example: 'Foolish reflections on work, rest and play'. Foolish? Come on! There's nothing foolish about it at all. This is downright down-to-earth common-sense, and it contains much more wisdom than I've encountered in a long time. If we could learn to live by even a tenth of this 'foolishness' the world would be a measurable more sensible place.

And then there's all those protestations about how John is not a theologian. Come off it! This is real theology; not a load of professors examining the Ugaritic ur-text and the writings of St Basil and arguing about what this Hebrew word actually means, but good honest reflections on the Bible in the context of real life and real-life ministry. This book makes it abundantly clear that John has read widely, experienced deeply and reflected thoughtfully and, as if further proof were needed, it's got some Greek in it. Not a theologian? John, you want to get out more, son!

And another thing: he calls himself a clown. Well excuse me, but I thought the idea of clowns was to make people laugh. So why did I read parts of this book with tears in my eyes? OK, there are funny bits (most of the book, come to think of it), but there's real depth here, and plenty of the kind of poignancy that comes from talking about the very real pains and tragedies of life. If you think this book is the Christian equivalent of a custard pie in the face, you've been well and truly conned.

So my advice to you, if you've picked up this book wondering whether or not it's worth buying, is this: buy it immediately, read it carefully, enjoy it immensely (that part won't be difficult), try to live it out and then see how much you can sue the publishers for under the Trades Description Act.

John Leach
Anglican Renewal Ministries

INTRODUCTION

I am not a theologian; I'm a clown.

So if you picked this book up looking for something wise you could be looking in the wrong place. There are only foolish reflections in here. I never could quite get the hang of all that academic stuff they teach you at university and college.

I'm not knocking it mind you – some of my best friends are clever. But I'm not. I'm foolish and that's the way I like it. In fact, I think it's the way God made me. Oh, I've tried to be clever. I'm good at pretending and quite a few people get taken in. I've got a few letters after my name and 'Revd.' in front so some people think I'm important. I've got a good imagination too and my peculiar memory helps me to know one or two facts about a lot of things so when I'm really on form I can impress people at social gatherings with my so-called 'wisdom'. But the truth is I'm a fool. I'm bald and overweight and the wrinkly side of forty and I know I can't hold a candle to most of the guys (and ladies) who write books.

Now don't get the idea I'm running myself down. I don't have a problem with self-esteem. If anything I have rather an excess of personality. No, I'm just stating the facts so you're not misled. I don't want anyone writing to me saying they were expecting 'wisdom'. I'm a clown, I tell you!

In my day job I get to speak regularly to crowds of people and help the lonely and the sad and the sick and the anxious to find a meaning in life. I get to do baptisms, weddings and funerals, visit old ladies and take school assemblies. I sometimes attend riveting meetings called PCCs and synods and of course I get to take loads of services. As an Anglican vicar in a wonderful parish with a terrific congregation I get the chance to help people make a difference. And, thanks be to God, I often get the chance to make a difference myself. But I think I'm happiest when I get into the multi-coloured jumpsuit, red wig and orange boots of Gof the Clown. You see what I mean; I really am a clown! Convinced yet?

So why write a book if I've got no words of wisdom and nothing clever to say? Well, I've thought about this carefully and I guess there's only one answer: God told me to. Well, *asked* me to actually and I said 'yes'. So here it is – *Prophetic Balloon Modelling*.

Why 'Prophetic Balloon Modelling'? Three reasons. One – it's a good catchy title that might grab your attention and encourage you to buy it. After all it's the kind of foolishness we clowns like to indulge in and I *do* like balloon modelling. Two – putting 'Prophetic' in the title gives it a kind of super-spiritual dimension and it's bound to attract the charismatic audience. A bit like 'Prophetic Intercession', 'Power Evangel-icalism', 'Anointed Sabbaticals' – you know the kind of thing I mean. (Oh, maybe you picked the book up for that reason? Don't let me put you off!)

Third reason? Well, you'll have to wait to the end of the book for the third reason. Now don't go skipping to the last chapter without reading the bits in between or it won't make sense. If you've read this far you've probably bought the book and you won't want to waste your money.

The subtitle is 'Foolish Reflections on Work, Rest and Play' so, as you might expect, there's quite a lot of that in the book. I've split it up into three sections entitled: Work, Play and Rest. (I did ask a certain chocolate bar manufacturer if they'd care to sponsor me but they politely declined so I'm afraid they won't be getting a mention.) I've got the idea that the right kind of balance between these three areas might just lead to the right kind of life, lived in the way that God wants.

Now please don't get the idea that I'm writing the book because *I've* managed to get the balance right. Although I'm a clown I still haven't learned how to juggle and as for balancing on a tightrope – forget it! And although I've been a parish priest for a good many years I'm pretty wobbly in that area too. Juggling and balancing are things I get to try a lot and I haven't mastered them yet.

For instance, I knew seven years ago that God wanted me to write a book on rest. The problem was I was just far too busy. Far too much work, far too little rest and certainly no time for play. And one other not so small matter to cope with: in 1981 after a severe bout of glandular fever and hepatitis I contracted ME and I have struggled with it on and off ever since. But more of that later in the book. The point I'm trying to make is that I am far from being any kind of expert. I'm not clever; I'm a fool. I'm not strong and healthy; I have chronic fatigue syndrome. And as I have already told you – I'm not a theologian, I'm a clown!

The book has taken quite a few years to write. Not because I can't quite manage joined-up writing yet but in the main because I never got round to

putting all the thoughts on paper (or word proces-
sor). Ah well, never put off until tomorrow what
you can do the next day, as they say. In the end it
took a much needed three months sabbatical to
give me the final prod. During the summer of 1998
I was able to 'work' in Colorado Springs, 'play' in
California and Medicine Hat, and 'rest' in the Isle
of Mann. I'm really thankful to all the people I met
on that fabulous pilgrimage, especially to the apos-
tolic leaders at the World Prayer Centre conference
and all the wonderful participants at Clown Camp.
You taught me so much and, along with my family
and friends, helped me to interweave the three elements that comprise the main essence of this book.
Some of my clowning became rest and some of my
church growth conference became play.

I thank God also for all the many individuals I
met on trains and planes, in airports and shops
who, in different ways, have contributed unknow-
ingly to this book and made me a better person by
touching my life with theirs. It is often the little
people, the anonymous and apparently unremark-
able, who make the most impact. God sees them all
and he knows!

This is not a book that provides a lot of answers.
It's not a book on time management, stress management or child management. There are plenty of
much better books on those subjects; some of the
titles of which you'll find at the end. This is just a
book of foolish reflections. I was too busy to write
a book on work, too preoccupied to write a book on
play and too tired to write a book on rest. This is a
book on balloons. This may not be a great book but
I've tried to pour myself into these foolish
thoughts. It may not win any awards but, as Bart

Simpson so famously confessed: *'Part of this D minus belongs to God!'*

So now I've got all the explanations and excuses out of the way I'd better get on with the book. I'm more grateful than I can say to a whole crowd of people for giving me the time, space and resources to write, think and pray. To the wonderful congregation at St Margaret's, Stanford-*the*-Hope, whose love and encouragement never ceases to amaze me. To Barbara for proof reading, to Marjorie (my GDB!) for all her help and to Janice, my magnificent colleague. To my Prayer Shield (Caroline, Brian, Maureen, Pat, Sue W., Terry, Maria, Sue D. Sylvia, Ron, Peggy, Thelma, John, Coral, Martin, Uta, Ken, Hazel, Val and Barbara) whose steadfast intercession holds back the hosts of darkness and makes the way clear for us to advance the Kingdom. To David and my publishers at Eagle for having confidence in a holy fool and to my dear aunt, Gwen, for giving me an incomparable environment in which to write. To my dear family, Mother, Father and Peter, who are always there for me and give me so much. To my children, Ben and Hannah, who make me old and keep me young: I'm so proud of you both and I want everyone to know that. To Kim, wife, lover, friend and counsellor – you were rightly named 'golden'. Thank you for helping me look beyond the gift to the Giver.

And to you, the reader. Thanks for picking up the book. I hope you get as much pleasure from reading it as I did from writing it. May you find purpose in your work, fun in your play and peace in your rest.

Above all I want to give thanks and praise to my Special Friend, Jesus – Saviour, Lord and God. Your grace and mercy are overwhelming. Thank you for saving me and for giving me so much and so many to share it with.

All this is for You, Jesus. My crown is at your feet.

How to Make a Balloon Model

You do know how to make a balloon model, don't you? You don't? Well, watch closely and I'll explain. There are three stages to the process: the hard bit, the fun bit and the easy bit. You'll need a pure white latex modelling balloon (No. 260Q) because we're going to make a dove, a symbol of the Holy Spirit. Ready? OK, take a deep breath.

The hard bit. First you inflate the balloon. Half a dozen good puffs should do it. Yes, I did say this was the hard bit! It could take you quite a bit of work to get this stage right. Alternatively, to save your lungs you could use a balloon pump. Once the balloon is inflated there are three important things you have to remember. First – leave a bit of

←Approx 3in→

space at the end of the balloon. That bit of space at the end is very important. Second – let a bit of air out to relieve the pressure slightly. Letting out that little bit of air is also important. Third – don't let go but tie off the end of the balloon in a neat little knot. It's very important to hold onto your balloon and not let the air out. OK so far? Now you're ready to model your dove.

The fun bit. Six good twists are all you need to transform your white modelling balloon into a beautiful dove – symbol of the Holy Spirit. Actually, this is so simple: it's child's *play*. Pinch in

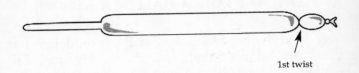

1st twist

an inch from the nozzle (knotted) end and twist. Make three more twists two and a half inches apart then cross the fourth twist over the first and twist

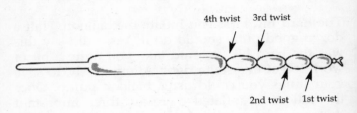

4th twist   3rd twist

2nd twist   1st twist

them together. You should now have a kind of triangle and about a two-foot length of balloon left. The triangle is the tail. Make a ten inch loop and put your fifth twist around twists one and four and then make another ten inch loop and put your sixth and final twist also around twists one and four. These are the wings. Finally – and this is the crucial

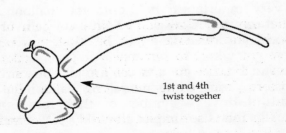

1st and 4th twist together

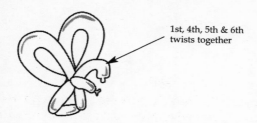

1st, 4th, 5th & 6th
twists together

bit – pinch the little bit of balloon at the nipple end between your thumb and forefinger and pull it down whilst gently squeezing the last couple of

inches of the balloon. The effect is to make the dove's head and beak. Voila! Now, wasn't that fun? (You may find by this time that you've attracted quite a crowd of spectators who would all like to see what you are doing.) Now – here comes the best bit.

The easy bit. Now you've finished your balloon model you can take a *rest*. But first, you need to give your dove to someone you love. Better still; give it to someone you *don't* love. Then sit back, take six deep breaths, relax and watch what happens.

You don't have to be a clown to understand this, but if you are it helps!

One thing I do
(Philippians 3)

Work
What we have to do

'My whole life is "have to"!'
Steve Martin (*Parenthood*)

'Do not work for food that spoils, but
for food that endures to eternal life . . .'
Jesus (John 6:27)

FIRST PUFF:
HAVE TO, LIKE TO, NEED TO?

A man was once asked if he'd lived in a particular area all his life. 'Not yet,' was the swift response!

I've lived over forty years in various places and rubbed shoulders with a whole variety of different people, but I haven't lived all my life yet. When I have and they lay me in the ground I'd like Paul's words from 2 Timothy 4 verse 7 to be put on my stone: *'I have fought the good fight, I have finished the race, I have kept the faith.'*

Then again, I might just have them put: 'I told you I was ill!'

In the meantime I'm *living* my life, trying the best I can to make a difference. Often, my life is more driven than led: compelled by strong desires and trying to live up to others' expectations. I try to be a good father and husband and often fail. I long to see my church grow and forget several times that it's God's responsibility and not mine. I worry about what people think about me and whether I'll make the grade. I guess I'm no different from you. Happily, the clown in me keeps me from taking myself too seriously, and my family and friends are very adept at overlooking my weaknesses.

Rhythm, Shape and Balance

Life has a lot to do with rhythm and balance; we were designed to be integrated beings: body, mind and spirit. This is no new concept since we have realised for centuries the importance of harmony in our lives. There are a whole variety of suggestions for achieving it, from exercise and diet programmes to Eastern mysticism. These foolish thoughts are not aiming to compete with those ideas. There are plenty of books that do that. If what follows makes you think and, even better, if it makes you smile, then I shall be happy.

It seems to me that the three main areas that make up our lives are Work, Rest and Play. Most 24-hour periods contain elements of all three. Eight hours of sleep seems to be the optimum, and the 'eight-hour day' seems to be the recommended work period. The remaining eight hours will be filled with a variety of other activities which may include things as diverse as eating, watching TV, making love, dancing, worshipping God, washing-up, building model aircraft, mowing the lawn, reading etc., as well as other elements of work, rest and play. It seems clear to me that there is a need for a balance between these three major areas. I am certainly not the first to espouse this view. The Puritan, Richard Rogers, believed that a day should consist of eight hours of work, eight for sleeping and eight for relaxation; the latter including time with friends, reading and enjoying God's creation.

There will undoubtedly be times when work is regularly more or less than eight hours: for the overworked and the unemployed. There will also be times when sleep is more or less than eight hours: for the insomniac and the bedbound. It will also be true that there will be times throughout our lives when one of the three areas will be more prominent. As children we will spend more time in play. As we grow older work will feature more prominently. Following retirement we may well find that, willingly or unwillingly, rest will be more important.

We need to know what to do and when to do it. Maybe, in the tangled web of our lives we can seek to find a balance that makes sense of it all. What we have to do, what we like to do and what we need to do may yet provide a dynamic equilibrium to enable a more fulfilled and focussed life that can be truly *lived*.

Some years ago Groucho Marx asked Woody Allen what he would like people to be saying about him in a hundred years time. Woody replied, *'Doesn't he look good for his age!'* I'm not going to live forever (not on earth, at least), but when I'm gone I would like people to say that, in the main, I got the balance about right.

The Working Class

In a recent survey conducted by ICM for Radio 4's *Today* programme, 1,178 people selected at random were asked what class they considered themselves to be: 41 per cent said they considered themselves to be middle class, 1 per cent said they considered themselves to be upper class and 55 per cent said they considered themselves to be working class. (Presumably, 3 per cent didn't know or put 'other'!) Even people in managerial positions said they considered themselves to be working class. With the huge advances in information communication technology, vastly increased choice and the enormous opportunities available for people in the Western world, our preoccupation with work is fascinating. It is the one factor that influences the major part of our adult lives and, despite the caricature of an idle workman leaning on a shovel we are, in the main, obsessed with work.

One of my favourite films is the excellent *Parenthood,* starring Steve Martin. It is warm, moving, hilariously funny and bitingly insightful on the meaning of life, family and relationships. At one point, Martin, playing the harassed father who's just quit his job as an advertising executive only to discover his wife is pregnant, heads out of the door for yet another commitment. They need to discuss their future but there's just no time to talk. 'Do you have to go?' his wife pleads with him. The desperate man pokes his head round the door with a look that conveys all the pain and frustration of an ordinary life, over-stressed and over-stretched. *'My whole life is "have to"!'* he says.

Feeling that your whole life is 'have to' is not something peculiar to a character in a film, I'm sure. Many, if not most of us have felt at times that we are marching to the beat of someone else's drum and that we have little control over the direction of our lives. This loss of control and not even having the opportunity to pause and reflect on what we have just worked on, makes our work lose its meaning and presses us further into stress and anxiety.

Managing Pressure

'Stress' is one of the great buzzwords of the late twentieth century and it seems to me that it grows inexorably out of a life where we 'have to'. We 'have to' live and in order to live we 'have to' eat and in order to eat we 'have to' earn and in order to earn we 'have to' work. Work then is the thing we 'have to' do. The result is that we often feel driven by forces outside our control. We find ourselves like hamsters racing round in a wheel but with no opportunity to jump off. Worse still, we reach a kind of limbo where we are burnt out and listless, lacking in passion and purpose, having long ago lost the reason for what we are doing. We work hard but we are never satisfied; we never discover the true pleasure that comes from a job well done. We rush from place to place, filling our lives with more and more business and busyness and occasionally we ask ourselves what it's all for. At times of more desperate humour we wonder if when we're dead they'll inscribe on our tombstone: 'Gone to *another* meeting'!

Tim La Haye, in his book, *How to Manage Pressure before Pressure Manages You*, notes how many directors and leaders of large companies suffered bankruptcy, severe illness or even suicide. '*All these men*,' he writes, '*had learned the art of making a living, but apparently none of them had learned how to live.*'[1]

Awareness of the dangers of stress seems to do little to alleviate it in the majority of us. Yes, I too have read books and papers on stress and I've been to seminars on how to manage it. Goodness, I've even preached sermons on it – whole series in fact! I've noted the increasing interest in awaydays and retreats (Christian and secular), all designed to soothe away those stresses and strains and get your life back into focus. My observation is that, even for those who make it a habit to regularly relax and 'de-stress', the call to go back to the things we 'have to' do grows ever more overwhelming. Consequently, for a great number of us in busy jobs and with growing families, and for a great number of us with little or no jobs and living alone, stress and burnout, passionlessness and inertia are a constant threat.

In the wonderful *Les Miserables* the desperate and disillusioned Fantine sings: '. . . *life has killed the dream I dreamed.*' Many of us begin life dreaming dreams and hoping hopes; building castles in the air and imagining all the great things we are going to achieve. How quickly those hopes can die and those dreams lie mired in the mud of dull routine as our days and years fill up with all the things we 'have to' do.

The Archbishop of Canterbury's Lent book for 1998 was *The Shape of Living* by David Ford.[2] In it Professor Ford talks about the 'multiple overwhelmings' of life. Moving out from the Old Testament example of the prophet Ezekiel, overwhelmed by God at the Kebar River, he examines the many things in life that overwhelm us, both good and bad. Chapter by chapter he looks at relationships, vocation and compulsion, discipline, suffering and death, and finally the feasting and celebration that comes through the overwhelming of the Resurrection.

Professor Ford begins his book with some examples of being overwhelmed, from something glorious like the sight of the Canadian Rockies to something frustrating like getting to grips with a new computer User Manual. I can relate to that. I remember, not so very long ago, gazing out across the Horseshoe Falls at Niagara, tears streaming down my face as I was literally overwhelmed by the glorious majesty of it all. And I recall all too well trying to make sense of my first computer User Manual, supposedly designed for the 'layman', and finding the contemplation of its functions and abilities, its megabytes and multitasking methods, an incomprehensible overwhelming.

David Ford encourages his readers to accept their experience of being overwhelmed – to first name it, then describe it (if that is possible) and then explore the resources for coping with it. In this way we begin to forge the shape of our lives.

Learning to Balance

The contention of *Prophetic Balloon Modelling* is not that work, stress-building and overwhelming as it may be, is something to be shunned or marginalised but that, properly understood and balanced with rest and play, it may begin to establish a balance or focus for our lives. It's a bit like learning to ride a unicycle or walk a slackrope. In the process we may fall off many times and even hurt ourselves quite badly but with perseverance and determination we finally discover our sense of balance.

Two important lessons can be gleaned from these examples. First – we cannot take our balance for granted. We need constantly to be realigning and readjusting which, if properly understood, brings excitement and wonder. Second – the falling off, and *even the pain of hurting ourselves* is an absolutely vital part of the whole exercise. Almost everything of value that we learn, we learn by 'falling off'. That is why I have no major concerns about not being a so-called 'expert' in the areas of work, rest and play.

I haven't yet mastered the art of riding a unicycle or walking a slackrope but I do know how to fall off. And, even more important – I know how to get up again! You don't have to be a clown to understand this, but if you are it helps!

In this section of the book I want to explore some of the 'have to' parts of our lives and see what can be discarded and what can be redeemed. I would like to encourage you, the reader, to examine the 'shape' of your own life: the balance you struggle to maintain and the stresses that overwhelm you. We're going to take a look at the amazing growth of information technology, choice overload, task-orientation and goal setting, work that stimulates and satisfies and work that overwhelms and destroys. And we will try to make sense of it all and attach value and purpose to it.

Work: Its Values and Hazards

Please understand that when I talk about 'work' in this section I am not merely talking about paid employment. I intend work to be seen in its widest context, although I fully realise that it is often the absence of paid employment that is so destructive of people's self-confidence and itself a source of great stress.

A while ago I discovered that there are four categories of 'employment' recognised by Her Majesty's Tax Inspectors. They are Employed, Self-Employed, Unemployed and . . . wait for it: the Clergy! So perhaps after all, us funny little guys in penguin outfits do have something unique to contribute to the job market, even if we do only work one day a week!

In a recent *Panorama* documentary for BBC 1 the serious risks of 'workaholism' were explored. Today more than six million people work more than forty-eight hours a week, as opposed to two million in the mid 1980s. Over one million of these work more than sixty hours a week. The programme looked at a number of individuals adversely affected by long working hours yet the point was made that many *enjoyed* a busy life in the office. Professor Gary Cooper of Manchester University said: 'People feel they *have* to be there' (my emphasis).

We work longer hours in England than anywhere else in Europe but in September of 1998 the British Government introduced a new Employment Time Directive that allows individuals to refuse to work more than forty-eight hours a week without prejudice to their job security or promotion prospects. Employment Rights Lawyer, Steven Cavalier, asserted that everyone would have the opportunity to put their own limit on the amount of hours people worked but suggested that not everyone would want to. *Panorama* interviewed a classic 'workaholic' who seemed to enjoy the challenge of pushing himself to the limit. He was accustomed to leaving his home at 6.00 am and not returning home before 9.00 pm. An average day would consist of twelve to fifteen hours of intensive work in a firm whose sales targets had doubled in the year. On the day the cameras followed him he had fifty e-mails to read and reply to before going home! Despite the £50,000 salary plus huge bonuses, he said it was not the money that drove him but his 'career aspirations'. At home his wife, who had given up her 'work' to look after their son, complained that at times he was tense and irritable, aggressive and aloof. He also suffered from recurrent headaches and became pale and drawn.

Another 'workaholic' – female this time – complained of stress and acne. She also had headaches and at one time, her hair began to fall out. Working in a busy London bank, dealing with millions of pounds every day, her family was never quite sure when they would see her at night. 'Mum goes mad when she comes in,' say her children. 'She moans because the dinner is cold.' In addition to health dangers, the effect of long working hours on time spent with children has been considerable. It is clear that the more hours parents work the less likely they are to spend time with their children. Two thirds of those working over forty-eight hours a week said that most days they don't even speak to their children!

In a survey of 1,000 people by Harris for The Institute of Personnel and Development, 72 per cent said they enjoyed work and didn't mind long hours, 84 per cent said they were satisfied with life and only 16 per cent feared dismissal. However, one third confessed to being workaholics and said they were more committed to work than to life at home. Professor Cooper said:

> I believe that the effect of long working hours on family life is extremely detrimental. It effects communication and leads to disturbed families, separation and divorce. We already have a very high divorce rate: the highest in Europe. This is not unrelated to long working hours.

Despite the satisfaction brought about by the increased money that often results from longer working hours, the most detrimental effects are seen when people are obliged to work long hours in occupations they do not like. One individual working an average of sixty to seventy hours a week (and occasionally ninety!) for a retail chain, suffered a heart attack at forty-four. Two years later he is still trying to recover his health. Whilst working these long hours he earned just £11,000 a year and often struggled to get a day off.

Being forced to work without any real job satisfaction appears to be a major contributor to stress and health problems. Those who do not have control over what they do are at highest risk and women appear to suffer most in this area. An acknowledged expert in the field, Professor Gian Carlo Di Renzo, observed that in women working more than forty hours a week there was a 70 per cent increased risk of premature birth. One of the women interviewed said: 'I know you should really rest more – take it easy – I've never done that. Never had the chance to.'

It's plain we 'have to' work and that compulsion is at its worst when it is imposed from outside. Often, however, we make the decision ourselves and choose to take the risks with our health, our relationships and our lives. Someone said it is like winding up a clock, turning the mechanism tighter and tighter. What happens when the spring will go no further? Unquestionably, we will need a whole range of resources to help us to make sense of this complex area.

One group that has been set up recently to sup-

port Christians in the workplace is the WorkNe
partnership. Its specific aim is 'to connect, equip
and resource you as a Christian in the workplace s
that you can integrate your faith with your worl
and effectively communicate it to others'.

Jesus said that we need to work not for food tha
spoils but for what endures, even to eternity
'Work', rather than mere employment, can be an
activity (even for the jobless) that brings encouragement, fun, value and purpose. Work can pro
vide the road that leads to destiny. Despite its haz
ards it can be imbued with vision, passion and
hope.

SECOND PUFF:
AS SOON AS THE RUSH IS OVER

There's a magic toilet in my house – really! It's incredible. Whenever I go in there and particularly when I reach the point of, shall we say, no return – the phone rings. On really magical days the doorbell goes at the same time. The strange thing is that there was a magic toilet in my last house too. I've heard a rumour that they are a peculiar feature of parsonages and there is often a similar magical quality to the bath/shower, usually when you are covered in soap and have shampoo in your eyes. You may have encountered these phenomena yourself and have wondered at it.

Murphy's Law
Research in this area has led me to the conclusion that it is related, at least in part, to a man called Murphy and can be crystallised into a general maxim that states: 'Anything that can go wrong will go wrong.' Here are some more of Murphy's laws, with which you may be familiar:

Constants aren't, variables do.
No good deed goes unpunished.
Leak-proof seals – will.

Self-starters – will not.

Interchangeable parts – won't.

If you try to please everybody, nobody will like it.

A short cut is the longest distance between two points.

You will always find something in the last place you look.

The chance of a piece of toast falling with the buttered side down is directly proportional to the cost of the carpet.

No matter how long or hard you shop for an item, after you've bought it, it will be on sale somewhere cheaper.

The other line always moves faster.

In order to get a loan you must first prove you don't need it.

Any tool dropped whilst repairing a car will roll underneath to the exact centre.

The repairman will never have seen a model quite like yours before.

In any hierarchy, each individual rises to his or her own levels of incompetence and then remains there.

The light at the end of the tunnel is the head-lamp of an oncoming train.

All warranties expire upon payment of invoice.

If more than one person is responsible for a mis-calculation, no one will be at fault.

There is always one more bug.

I can almost imagine you nodding your head sadly as you read the above. You've probably had the same experience as me! Mind you, there may be ways to get round Murphy's law. What if you tied the toast to the back of a cat before you dropped it? However, bemoaning the fact that we are victims of strange and unavoidable laws is not the whole story by any means. How we handle time, for example, can determine whether we will be rushed or rested.

Busy, Busy, Busy

Being a clown means that I am a truthspeaker and I have to be honest when I say there are some days when I feel there isn't time to blow my nose. It's crazy really because I'm supposed to be the person others come to when they are stressed out or too busy to rest or too serious to play. As a priest I am the one with the answers, the one who can hand out the right medicine to treat the condition – at least that's how it's thought to be. Vicars are some-how supposed to be a combination of a thoroughly 'together' kind of executive and a sort of super-holy monk, immersed in prayer and contempla-tion. If you are a vicar reading this (and when you've stopped laughing hysterically) you'll know what an utterly false impression this is. Most of the vicars I know, even the good ones, are rushed off their feet workaholics, often with neglected fami-lies and partners who are at best resigned and at worst bitter and very angry with the church.

I used to have an Argos poster fixed to the door of my study that went something like this:

As soon as the rush is over
I'm going to have a nervous breakdown.
I've worked for it; I owe it to myself
And no one is going to deprive me of it.

I'm happy to say I took that poster down some time ago. For one thing it was too close to the truth and for another the longer it stayed there the more chance there was of it becoming a self-fulfilling prophecy. Well, I've managed to avoid the nervous breakdown but I'm still far from learning the secret of properly balanced work. Like some many-headed monster it still takes bites out of me and, worse still, out of my family and friends. The world of work continues to expand, growing in both amount and speed. We see symptoms of its effects in all aspects of life. Breakfast television has been with us for many years and we seldom see the test card now since the advent of 24-hour viewing. Even on Radio 4, that doyen of respectability, scheduling has been changed to accommodate changing work patterns and programmes begin half an hour earlier in the day.

In our technology driven, push-button world, the pace of life hurtles forward with a momentum that would give our grandparents the vapours! In the wake of this speeding phenomenon lie the damaged lives of many who have fallen prey to the rush to achieve more and more and the inevitable pressures of the modern world. In America (home of the analyst) the Holmes-Rahe scale has been widely recognised as a helpful indicator of stress factors. The numbers in the right hand column indicate the degree of stress associated with each event (left column). When we add together the values of the events relating to our lives in the last twelve months we have an indication of our stress level. A score of 200 or more means you are in danger of some kind of breakdown.

HOLMES-RAHE SCALE [1]
(Revised by Keith W. Sehnert)

1.	Death of spouse	100
2.	Divorce	73
3.	Marital separation	65
4.	Jail term	63
5.	Death of close family member	63
6.	Personal injury or illness	53
7.	Marriage	50
8.	Fired at work	47
9.	Marital reconciliation	45
10.	Retirement	45
11.	Change in health of family member	44
12.	Pregnancy	40
13.	Sex difficulties	39
14.	Gain of new family member	39
15.	Business readjustment	39
16.	Change in financial state	38
17.	Death of a close friend	37
18.	Change to a different line of work	36
19.	Change in the number of arguments with spouse	35
20.	Mortgage over $40,000	31
21.	Foreclosure of mortgage or loan	30
22.	Change in responsibilities at work	29
23.	Son or daughter leaving home	29
24.	Trouble with in-laws	29
25.	Outstanding personal achievement	28
26.	Spouse begins or stops work	26
27.	Begin or end school	26
28.	Change in living conditions	25
29.	Revision of personal habits	24
30.	Trouble with the boss	23

31.	Change in work hours or conditions	20
32.	Change in residence	20
33.	Change in schools	20
34.	Change in recreation	19
35.	Change in church activities	19
36.	Change in social activities	18
37.	Mortgage or loan of less than $40,000	17
38.	Change in number of family get-togethers	15
39.	Change in sleeping habits	15
40	Change in eating habits	15
41.	Single person living alone	–
42.	Other – describe	–
43.	Other – describe	–

TOTAL

If the exercise itself is not too stressful (!) you might like to add up your own score. A number of very interesting factors emerge from a study of the scale, not least of which are the stressful areas that are work-related. It is also interesting to note that the scale was devised almost twenty years ago. I can think of a few items to add to the scale myself, like listening to the inane music at the other end of the phone whilst being put on 'hold', trying to fill in your tax form and attempting to re-programme your video recorder. There must be a few extra points in that! Even writing a book appears to carry with it a stress factor: so much for my efforts!

Jesus and Stress
Even with all the points I've accrued from the above scale, I still consider myself one of the lucky ones. I think of the church leaders I know who have fallen prey to breakdown and burnout or

whose marriages have disintegrated, leaving damaged families and wounded congregations. Others
still have fallen to the temptations of money, sex
and power, contributing stacks of copy to the
tabloids only too willing to exploit yet another
'vicar runs off with choir mistress/master/boy'
headline.

I don't know whether it's worse in the market
place than in the church, I just know that the
church doesn't have the answers to the problems of
overwork, stress and burnout because it is unable
to practise what it purports to preach. From my
reading of the Gospels it doesn't appear that Jesus
was any less susceptible to the pressures of daily
life and work, in fact probably much more so. Let's
join him for a moment by the side of Lake Galilee:

> Jesus withdrew with his disciples to the lake,
> and a large crowd from Galilee followed. When
> they heard all he was doing, many people came
> to him from Judea, Jerusalem, Idumea, and the
> regions across the Jordan and around Tyre and
> Sidon. Because of the crowd he told his disciples
> to have a small boat ready for him, to keep the
> people from crowding him. For he had healed
> many, so that those with diseases were pushing
> forward to touch him.

> (Mark 3:7–10)

Listen – that was some crowd! And all demanding
Jesus' individual attention. And it appears this was
the norm for Jesus' ministry. Very little time to be
on his own. Crowds of people everywhere he went.
He sets off across the lake for a picnic with his
friends; when he reaches the other side – crowds of

people! He's trying to take a quiet lunch at a friend's place; who comes banging on the door? – crowds of people! Even when he goes up into the hills for five minutes peace with his Father the disciples come looking for him with more needs and demands. In Mark 6 we read of him advocating '*some rest*' to his disciples and together they go off secretly in the boat to 'a solitary place'. But someone spills the beans and when he gets there what does he find? You've guessed it – crowds of people!

In the passage above we read that there were so many people Jesus didn't have room to stand on the shore but had to get into the boat on the lake. You may think Jesus was able to let this all wash over him. After all he was God, wasn't he? But let's not forget he was human as well as divine, subject to the same tiredness, frustration and temptation as us. One version of the Bible says Jesus got into the boat and told the disciples to push off. I don't think I'm being disrespectful to him to say I think there must have been times that Jesus felt like telling the crowds of people to 'push off' as well.

The more we read Jesus' life story the more we realise here was a man who somehow had work, rest and play in the right balance. His life was focused; he had a clear purpose. 'As long as it is day,' he said, 'we must do the work of him who sent me' (John 9:4). Later he told Pontius Pilate, 'for this reason I was born, and for this I came into the world, to testify to the truth' (John 18:37). In the church and in the market place so many of us are working without purpose, just occasionally stopping to ask ourselves what it is all for, but seldom finding the truth.

Margin

I think it is probably a subdivision of Murphy's dogma that says the amount of work always expands to fill the time available in which to do it. In his devastatingly insightful book, *The Sixty Minute Father*, Rob Parsons has a brilliant comment on his 'One Second Page' that has an application far beyond parenting skills. It simply states: 'Remember "The greatest illusion of all" and believe . . . The slower day is not coming!'[2] I guess we've all heard ourselves saying: 'When I get to the weekend I'll take a break', 'I'll get a rest during the summer', 'We'll do it when this or that is paid off'. We think that some time in the future there will be an easier or quieter moment when we can evaluate, reassess; take a break. In the New Year . . . when the kids leave home . . . when I retire. The sad truth Rob Parsons outlines is that this day never arrives. We constantly postpone the kind of life decisions, or even simple breaks in our time, that would allow us the right kind of balance of work, rest and play. As Rob Parsons wisely observes: nobody on his or her deathbed ever said: 'I wish I'd spent more time at the office.'

Breaks in time don't always have to be huge; planned weeks in advance and organised down to the last detail. Holidays themselves can be even more stressful, at times, than work. In fact, if we run our lives from one large break to the next, working in between as though we have to earn the time we take off, we defeat the purpose entirely. In my experience, breaks are best when they are spread throughout our work: little and often. They're like the small space that it is so important to leave at the nipple end of the balloon. Of course,

longer breaks such as days off and vacations are
also important but, if we neglect the small times,
we are heading for trouble. Like a balloon full of
too much air with nowhere to go, it only takes just
a bit more pressure and: bang!

Another way of describing small breaks in time
is 'margins'. One of the best books I have read on
this subject is by the American physician, Richard
A. Swenson. It is called, simply, *Margin*.

> Marginless is being thirty minutes late to the
> doctor's office because you were twenty min-
> utes late getting out of the hairdresser's because
> you were ten minutes late dropping the children
> off at school because the car ran out of gas two
> blocks from the gas station – and you forgot
> your purse . . . Marginless is not having time to
> finish the book you're reading on stress; margin
> is having the time to read it twice. Marginless is
> fatigue; margin is energy. Marginless is red ink;
> margin is black ink. Marginless is hurry; margin
> is calm. Marginless is anxiety; margin is securi-
> ty. Marginless is culture; margin is countercul-
> ture. Marginless is reality; margin is remedy.
> Marginless is the disease of the 1990s. Margin is
> its cure.[3]

We can all relate to that, can't we? We've all found
ourselves in the position of trying to force the
fabled quart into the pint pot. Our margins are constantly being eroded as we desperately try to do
more or at least to do it quicker. I heard one evangelist say that he'd got himself so busy and
stressed he'd go into the toilet, flush it, and then
come out without doing what he went in for! Dr

Swenson describes living without 'margins' as overloading our limits. It is easy to see in terms of physical limits; we know that, as much as we might want to, we cannot travel from London to New York in five minutes nor can we get fifteen desks in an office only designed for two. Performance, emotional and mental limits are a lot harder to assess and here lies the danger. We may push ourselves to do with less sleep or seek to carry the problems of a host of others. Choice and information overload is also a great contributor to personal stress. We shall look at this in more detail in the next chapter.

One of the greatest causes of overload is the inability many of us have to use the simple word 'no'. If there are two things we have to do that can only be done at the same time then to one of those things we will have to say 'no'. It's amazing the knots we tie ourselves into, endeavouring to squeeze in more and more just so that we can avoid using that little word. We can leave that meeting early; perhaps we can delay the beginning of that appointment. We can take a short cut, drive faster, get up earlier, go to bed later or just plain work harder. Why? Because we 'have to'? More than half a dozen puffs into the balloon could push the capacity beyond reasonable limits.

If we could just have the maturity to say: 'No, I'm afraid I can't do that' more often, it would make a big difference. Realising that we have physical, emotional, mental and volitional limits and seeking to do slightly less than we are able, instead of slightly more, would create the spaces in our lives necessary to avoid this nineties disease.

But how did we arrive at this place?

Visions of the Future

Thirty to forty years ago, as this country began to emerge from the post-Second World War years, futurists began to speculate about what the world would be like at the end of the twentieth century. Science-fiction writers penned fabulous tales of communities peopled with robots and spaceships to carry us to Mars. Many theorised that by the nineties the increase of 'labour-saving devices' would give us vastly increased leisure opportunities and we would therefore need to think what we were going to do with all this extra time.

We may smile as we look back, for hindsight, they say, is an exact science. The fact is that those so-called 'labour-saving devices' were wrongly named. Sure, the microwave cooks our meal in a quarter of the time of the post-war stove and in a fraction of the time needed by an open fire. Nowadays, instead of washing our clothes in the river or public wash-house, beating them on rocks and hanging them on lines to dry in the sun; we have the convenience of thrusting them into large metal cubes, which not only wash biologically and fabric condition but also dry, thus saving energy and hours of time. But what do we do with all this extra time? Do we engage in more leisure activities or cultivate the kind of in-depth relationships we enjoyed at the riverside? No, we generally use it to do more work!

In reality our vacuum cleaners, word processors, microwaves and tumbledriers should be called 'labour-enhancing devices' because that is what they do. A couple of years ago a worker in a local building contractors told me his firm now equipped their vans with fax machines in order to save time. About the same time Reuters, the international news agency, replaced their electronic mailing system because sending information around the world *in only three seconds* was too long. Nowadays mobile phones and e-mail are quite commonplace devices in individuals' everyday life. Why are these changes necessary? Quite simply, to save time, because 'time is money' and if you don't do it some other individual or company or international conglomerate will do it faster or better and you will be out of work. You 'have to' do it!

So much for the visions of the post-war futurists. In some ways it's as daft as the person who said that if they'd had a computer in 1878 it would have predicted that the current rate of increase in horse-drawn carriages in one hundred years would see the world nine feet deep in horse manure! The predictions of the sixties did not lead to a society where work was carried out by robots, and most people spent their days in leisure activities. True, the robots are here, in the shape of dishwashers, automated assembly lines and so on, but we also have what must be the greatest oxymoron in the world: the 'leisure industry'. How's that for a contradiction in terms! For many people leisure has become something that is fitted into a busy schedule or participated in not for the pleasure it evokes but because you're told you ought to do it. It has become only a means to an end and not something that can be enjoyed for its own sake. In this way it is little different from work. It is something else we 'have to' do.

In his fascinating book *Visions*, New York physicist Michio Kaku paints a mind-blowing picture of future scientific development.[4] Not for him the fanciful speculations of the sixties. Basing his theories on well-established scientific progress he charts the revolutions that have taken place in the fields of computers, biotechnology and quantum physics. He speculates on what changes will take place in the years leading up to 2020, to 2050 and to the twenty-second century. While it would be arrogant for a simple clown to question the superbly researched views of such an eminent scientist and communicator, I cannot help wondering how the evolution of work, rest and play will affect these momentous developments.

For as long as I can remember I have been an ardent fan of *Star Trek* (the term is 'Trekker' by the way, not 'Trekkie'!) and particularly *The Next Generation*. Jean-Luc Picard has long been a role model; we even have the same hairstyle! The fictional world of the Federation of Planets provides some equally fascinating visions of what a future society might be like. Professor Kaku himself refers to *Star Trek* as he sets out his theses. What intrigues me even more than the matter replicators, quantum torpedoes and warp-drive capabilities is the development of society and belief systems. The fictional world of the twenty-fourth century no longer uses any kind of money, has eradicated poverty and war on Earth and has made television obsolete. A major form of entertainment has become the holodeck, a further extension of virtual reality that allows absolute interaction between individual and computer which does not compromise safety but can stretch the bounds of ethics in a hypothetical environment. What is most interesting to me is the way in which these latter developments impinge upon interpersonal relationships. The writers, directors and actors of *Star Trek* are to be complimented on the way these relationships are explored and developed.

In the 1960s, speculation about the future did not include the views of any scientists. Today, *Visions* seems restricted to the views of only scientists, which is entirely fair since it is a thoroughly scientific work. I wonder if the additional hypotheses of philosophers, science-fiction writers, psychologists, priests and even clowns would provide a fuller and even more breath-taking picture. How different will work, rest and play be by the end of the next century and what effect will their evolution have upon society?

As soon as the rush is over, what space will be left I wonder?

THIRD PUFF:
TO BE OR NOT TO BE?

Ever since the eponymous (I've always wanted to use that word) Prince of Denmark asked the question 'to be or not to be?', and quite probably long before he asked it, people have been making similar enquiries about their existence. Mind you, I think Hamlet was asking what pencil he should use: 2B or not 2B? Pencils? Come on – wake up!

Choice and Overload
To be honest, choices have been with us since the Garden of Eden and now, as then, we usually make the wrong ones. Strange, isn't it, that in the beginning we had only one choice? To eat or not to eat! Adam and Eve, it appears, could do anything they liked in the garden. Picnics, walks, games of tag, discussions on the meaning of life. And probably every day they had a chance for a stroll and a chat with God. No worries about washing and ironing and no real anxieties about what the future would bring. Work was easy and unpressured, play was fun (well, what else would you expect from all that uninterrupted time with the partner of your dreams?) and rest was deep and restorative. All that and just one choice. We might wonder that

God gave us choice and free will in the first place. He could have designed us to always do the right thing; always make the right choice. It would certainly have saved him a lot of grief. But we wouldn't have been human beings then; we wouldn't have been made in his image.

The ability to choose is one of the great qualities that make us people and to take away or severely reduce that ability is to dehumanise us. Most of us, certainly those of us in the affluent West, have the opportunity to choose a whole variety of things from where we live and with whom we live, to what brand of margarine we buy and which soap opera we'll follow (or not!).

The other side of the coin is a rapidly expanding phenomenon known as 'choice overload'. Despite numerous pleas from my children I've consistently resisted the pressure to get satellite or cable television. The main reason (apart from the extra cost) is that I just couldn't cope with all the choices! It's hard enough to decide between the excellent costume drama on BBC 1, the premiere blockbuster on ITV and the rivetting Channel 4 nature presentation on the sex life of the bullfrog (I wonder if that should be 'ribetting'?). I just don't think I could mange having to choose between 100-plus other programmes beamed in from all over the place. Likewise, although I now use e-mail quite a lot, I tend to hold back from surfing the Internet. I just can't stand all those choices!

Now don't write me off as a technophobe or fuddy-duddy old traditionalist; choice overload is a real problem and it confronts us wherever we turn. In the supermarket we find ourselves faced with a dazzling array of choices and that's just for the baked beans! Time was when we asked the nice lady behind the counter at the corner shop for a pot of jam it was a simple choice of Hartleys or Robertsons. Now we have a choice of half a dozen manufacturers in this country and several from overseas. There are umpteen different flavours and combinations of flavours. There's low-sugar, no-sugar, low-fat, high bran, low-salt, high protein, seedless, rindless, mindless or fruitless. There's low-price, cut-price, special offer or two extra pots free if we buy the new experimental brand of mar-malade. Of course, that comes in 57 varieties too. How do we make a choice? Yet we all have to do it, day after day.

I find increasing numbers of sane, rational peo-ple agonising over choices, glued to TV monitors or hunched over keyboards because they are afraid they'll miss something or, faced with the number of options, make the wrong choice. We find ourselves wandering around shops and stores, taking hours to come to a decision and then coming out without anything, or worse, with something we don't real-ly want. Restaurant menus are getting bigger as varieties of food increase. In the past, meat and two veg were the general order of the day. You now get the option of jacket potatoes, rice (brown, basmati or fried), pasta, lentils, fries (used to be called 'chips'), and a bewildering array of other exotic vegetables and fruit, some of which sound as if they have come from a *Star Trek* replicator!

Now, don't get me wrong. Choice is a wonder-ful thing and its increase is a clear indication of a developing civilisation and the expansion of the global village. But like other things mentioned in this section it has to be handled carefully and properly balanced. Paranoia about choice and fear of decision making will not provide for a stable lifestyle. When it comes down to the wire the choice really is 'to be or not to be'. Being, after all, is a lot more important than doing. Not everyone has the chance to choose what he or she'll do but we can all choose what we'll be. It's no mistake that we are called human beings and not human doings!

Attitude is Everything

Choice about how we live our lives and the attitude we take can have a profound effect upon us and upon those around us. A positive approach can engender encouragement and enjoyment; a negative attitude only fosters self-centredness and depression. We choose at any given moment how we will react to people and situations we encounter. Here's a lovely story I picked up that amply illustrates the point:

Jerry was the kind of guy you love to hate. He was always in a good mood and always had something positive to say. When someone would ask him how he was doing, he would reply, 'If I were any better, I would be twins!'

He was a unique manager because he had several waiters who had followed him around from restaurant to restaurant. The reason the waiters followed Jerry was because of his attitude. He was a natural motivator. If an employee was having a bad day, Jerry was there telling the employee how to look on the positive side of the situation.

Seeing this style really made me curious, so

one day I went up to Jerry and asked him, 'I don't get it! You can't be a positive person all of the time. How do you do it?' Jerry replied, 'Each morning I wake up and say to myself, Jerry, you have two choices today. You can choose to be in a good mood or you can choose to be in a bad mood. I choose to be in a good mood. Each time something bad happens, I can choose to be a victim or I can choose to learn from it. I choose to learn from it. Every time someone comes to me complaining, I can choose to accept their complaining or I can point out the positive side of life. I choose the positive side of life.'

'Yeah, right, it's not that easy,' I protested. 'Yes it is,' Jerry said. 'Life is all about choices. When you cut away all the junk, every situation is a choice. You choose how to react to situations. You choose how people will affect your mood. You choose to be in a good mood or a bad mood. The bottom line: It's your choice how you live life.' I reflected on what Jerry said.

Soon thereafter, I left the restaurant industry to start my own business. We lost touch, but I often thought about him when I made a choice about life instead of reacting to it. Several years later, I heard that Jerry did something you are never supposed to do in a restaurant business: he left the back door open one morning and was held up at gunpoint by three armed robbers. While trying to open the safe, his hand, shaking from nervousness, slipped off the combination. The robbers panicked and shot him. Luckily, Jerry was found relatively quickly and rushed to the local trauma centre. After 18 hours of surgery and weeks of intensive care, Jerry was released from hospital with fragments of the bullets still in his body.

I saw Jerry about six months after the accident. When I asked him how he was, he replied, 'If I were any better, I'd be twins. Wanna see my scars?' I declined to see his wound, but did ask him what had gone through his mind as the robbery took place. 'The first thing that went through my mind was that I should have locked the back door,' Jerry replied. 'Then, as I lay on the floor, I remembered that I had two choices: I could choose to live, or I could choose to die. I chose to live.' 'Weren't you scared? Did you lose consciousness?' I asked. Jerry continued, 'The paramedics were great. They kept telling me that I was going to be fine. But when they wheeled me into the emergency room and I saw the expressions on the faces of the doctors and nurses, I got really scared. In their eyes I read, "He's a dead man." I knew I needed to take action.' 'What did you do?' I asked. 'Well, there was this big, burly nurse shouting questions at me,' said Jerry. 'She asked me if I was allergic to anything. "Yes," I replied. The doctors and nurses stopped working as they waited for my reply. I took a deep breath and yelled, "Bullets!" Over their laughter, I told them, "I am choosing to live. Operate on me as if I am alive, not dead." '

Jerry lived thanks to the skill of his doctors, but also because of his amazing attitude. I learned from him that every day we have the choice to live fully. Attitude, after all, is everything.

Choosing to *be* is all about the kind of people we

are; the attitude we choose to take; the personality we decide to develop. It's about character rather than capability: attitude rather than activity. If the work we devote ourselves to is a reflection of our positive attitude we will begin to see work as satisfying and purpose-focused and carry it out as part of a thoroughly balanced lifestyle. Work is important, but work is not all there is. We cannot allow our lives to be defined merely by what we *do*. You are not a solicitor, teacher, road sweeper, cleaner, grocer, parson, accountant etc. You are YOU! A human *being;* someone made in the image of God – the eternal 'I AM'. Choose to be who you are and take Jerry's attitude to heart.

Perhaps Hamlet has something to say to us all. I hear that there's a theory that says if you put an infinite number of monkeys on an infinite number of typewriters one of them would be bound eventually to type out the complete works of Shakespeare. Bob Newhart, the American comedian, performs a sketch where he speculates on what would happen if two guys were given the task of overseeing such an experiment. They wander around the monkeys, commiserating with the particularly slow ones. Then, suddenly, one of them cries out: 'Quick, look at this! This one seems to have written something famous.' *(He reads slowly)* 'To . . . be . . . or . . . not . . . to . . . be. That . . . is . . . the . . . gzrnenplatt!'

To be or not to be. That *is* the question. That is also the choice.

FOURTH PUFF:
RADIATORS AND DRAINS

The character of Jerry we looked at in the last chapter is sadly very uncharacteristic of most people we meet nowadays. Some of the folks you bump into are very downbeat; you'd think they'd made a deathbed confession to murder and got better. They behave like the only person in the street who didn't get a competition entry from *Reader's Digest*. My grandfather used to tell of an acquaintance who, when asked how he was, replied, *'Just waiting to die!'* When the latter met a colleague in the street one day he was informed: *'I think I've found your pipe.'* 'How did you know it was my pipe?' whined my grandfather's acquaintance. *'Oh,'* said the colleague, *'I went to pick it up and it moaned at me!'* I expect we all know people like that. Never satisfied; always complaining; always finding fault. If it isn't the government, it's the newspapers; if it isn't that, then it's the weather!

Blessing or Cursing

It's undoubtedly true that, regardless of our circumstances, we can choose how we will react. Dr Richard Swenson quotes a letter from Mrs Nguyen

Thi An (not her real name), the wife of a Vietnamese pastor, falsely imprisoned for his faith. Her words stand as a silent condemnation of all we who love to complain.

My Dear Friends,

. . . You know around here we are experiencing hardships, but we thank the Lord He is comforting us and caring for us in every way. When we experience misfortune, adversity, distress and hardship, only then do we see the real blessing of the Lord poured down on us in such a way that we cannot contain it.

We have been obliged recently to leave our modest apartment and for over two months have been living on a balcony. The rain has been beating down and soaking us. Sometimes in the middle of the night we are forced to gather our blankets and run to seek refuge in a stairwell.

Do you know what I do then? I laugh and I praise the Lord, because we can still take shelter in the stairwell. I think of how many people are experiencing much worse hardships than I am. Then I remember the words of the Lord, 'To the poor, O Lord, You are a refuge from the storm, a shadow from the heat' (Isaiah 25:4) and I am greatly comforted . . .

Our Father . . . is the One who according to the Scriptures does not break the bruised reed nor put out the flickering lamp. He is the One who looks after the orphan and the widow. He is the One who brings blessing and peace to numberless people.

I do not know what words to use in order to describe the love that the Lord has shown our family. I can only bow my knee and my heart and offer to the Lord words of deepest thanks and praise. Although we have lost our house and our possessions, we have not lost the Lord, and He is enough. With the Lord I have everything. The only thing I would fear losing is His blessing!

Could I ask you and our friends in the churches abroad to continue to pray for me that I will faithfully follow the Lord and serve Him regardless of what the circumstances may be?

As far as my husband is concerned, I was able to visit him this past summer. We had a 20-minute conversation that brought us great joy . . .

I greet you with my love.

Mrs Nguyen Thi An[1]

Few of us in the comfortable and affluent West can fail to feel humbled by her words. I remember with shame my complaints about lack of finance, dislike of various foods and clothes and my grumbling at the weather!

Faced with fresh air and nourishment, warm clothes and adequate shelter we still moan. Blessed with good health, a secure job and supportive friends, we still find ourselves complaining. 'Why me?' is the constant gripe, 'it's not fair!' An attitude that demands rights and a feeling that society owes us is what characterises many of us today.

I'm sorry to say that some of the worst examples of this kind of outlook come from churchgoers. From the faces on some of them you'd think they'd been baptised in vinegar. They hold out a hand – you don't know whether to shake it or wring it out.

They've always got something to complain about or to criticise.

I guess a lot of this is symptomatic of the 'why me?' culture we're living in at the moment. You know what it's like – just when you've worked hard and managed to get it all together you forget where you put it. You spend your life trying to do well and please everyone and in the end someone else gets all the credit.

The down side to this is that it's very easy to sink into a kind of pseudo-religious fatalism. Whatever will be, will be. Worse still, many of us take on that most deadly of attitudes: cynicism. I know of few things more destructive of life and love than that. I find lots of people, particularly a number of Christian leaders I'm sorry to say, who are so enmeshed in this attitude it has become a kind of uniform that they wear. Cynicism is unquestionably the enemy of true gratitude, enthusiasm and real worship. It means never letting on how you really feel, undermining hope and vision and questioning every good idea without proposing viable alternatives. Ultimately, it smothers love and makes life tedious and barren. If sarcasm is the lowest form of wit then cynicism must be the lowest form of witlessness.

Giving out or Sucking in

Comparing people like the Vietnamese pastor's wife and my grandfather's miserable acquaintance, the words 'radiators' and 'drains' spring to mind. I'm sure you know what I mean. Radiators are usually big and bright and highly visible. They may not be particularly good looking but when they're switched on and working properly they give off plenty of warmth. When you're feeling cold and miserable it's great to get close to a radiator and warm up. In chilly weather everyone wants to huddle round the radiator and when you've just come in from the cold and wet there's nothing quite like sitting, hands cupped round a warm drink, with your back up against the radiator. I'm so glad that there are people in the world that are just like radiators and proud to call some of them my friends.

On the other hand there are drains. As their name implies they just suck you dry. Any problem you've got theirs is worse. You've got a spot; they've got half a dozen. You've got a cold; they've got gastro-enteritis. You've broken your leg; they've broken both. And all the encouragement, support, counselling and time that you pour into them is swallowed up like it's flowing down a drain. The more you give the more they want you to. They are the drains and though they need help too I must confess I do try to avoid them.

The funny thing is that radiators and drains have one major attribute in common. They are both termini, occurring at the end of the water system; both receiving water from the central core. They just use the water in different ways; one drains it away, the other uses it to radiate out heat. Need I say more?

Out of Work

Work can itself be draining or radiating and frequently it will be both. When work is seen solely in terms of paid employment the absence of it can be horrifically draining. I spent five years as a vicar in the Toxteth area of Liverpool 8 and both my children were born in that wonderful city. Unemployment has long been a problem there and particularly in the early 1980s when 82 per cent of white people and 91 per cent of black people in some parts of my parish were out of work. In years gone by, when the docks were thriving, employment was high. Older people would talk of the days when, at knocking off time, the streets would be full of men heading home after a day's work, easily recognised as dockers by the kerchief at their neck and the metal hook on their belt. Those days are long gone. Most of the docks are dead. Men walk the streets or hang out in clubs and pubs that stay open twenty-four hours a day. Some turn to crime, robbing cars to feed a drug habit. More often than not they stay in bed or lounge at home watching endless videos. I daresay Liverpool 8 was not much different from other areas of high unemployment in the country. Without employment many people (and men in particular) have essentially lost their reason for living.

The trouble is we have created a society where people are defined by what they do and not by what they are. When two people meet – in a pub, on a train, at a bus stop – one of the first questions asked is: 'What do you do?' Again, I find this is particularly true of men. During a couple of months travelling North America in the summer of 1998 I would often meet people on planes or trains or in airport terminals and get into conversation. Inevitably, one of the first things discussed was what we were *doing* and almost the last thing was our names, who we *are*. Now, isn't that strange?

Given that what we do, what we achieve, is seen as so important, it is hardly surprising that when the ability to be 'gainfully employed' is taken away from us we begin to lose focus and direction. Everything around us stigmatises unemployment; there are special places for the unemployed, reduced rates to remind them of their state and Job Centres where, sadly, the 'unwaged' are sometimes patronised and further excluded. Small wonder that many people find it hard to retire or, when they do, find themselves turning up at the office again, only to find things have changed and they are now a minor embarrassment to former colleagues. Some don't really retire at all. If they're 'white collar' they take on consultancies, if they're 'blue collar' they get a little job at the filling station, the local school or in numerous charity outlets. It amounts to the same thing; only the money is different. We all need *authentication*. Gerald, in the smash hit movie *The Full Monty*, lives the lie that he is still working as an executive, heading off to work every day, even booking holidays with his wife but not telling her the terrible truth.

We need to work; without it our life becomes meaningless and empty. Experts say being made redundant is one of the major causes of stress, ranking close behind divorce and bereavement. Apart from stress it can lead to depression, illness, marital breakdown and even suicide.

I used to think 'Protestant Work Ethics' was a non-conformist assembly plant just outside Basildon. I see now how important the work ethic is in the development of our lives. David Ford examines this in his chapter on 'Shaping Time and Energy'. He writes: 'The global marketplace produces many casualties. There are the unemployed and also those who are constantly overworked.'[2]

Nowadays, they tell me, working in the city
(and London in particular) can be like a drug for
the young and upwardly mobile executive. They'll
endure anything: long hours, cramped conditions,
cut-throat tactics on the promotion ladder, even the
train journey from Southend to Fenchurch Street.
The amazing thing is that for many it is not primarily the highly lucrative salary these type of jobs
attract but just the incredible 'buzz' that comes
from it. Sadly, as with many other addictions, it can
lead to disaster. Scores of young executives are
burnt out before the age of thirty, leaving behind
them a string of broken relationships. The majority
of couples who come to me seeking remarriage
admit the primary reason for the breakdown of
their previous relationship was pressure of work
and too little quality time to spend together.

Work itself can 'radiate' or 'drain', and those
involved in it can do likewise. We all know people
in dead-end jobs or facing the constant draining
vacuum of unemployment. Even when work is
tedious, dangerous or highly pressured, we can
find purpose and release. Despite being out of
work and facing the continual disappointment of
unanswered letters, there are some things we can
do. I'm not suggesting these provide all the
answers and they won't make you smile as much
as a good promotion, a fat cheque or two weeks in
the Seychelles. These are foolish thoughts, as I've
said before. You don't have to be a clown to understand this, but if you are it helps!

The steps we can take to confront loss of enthusiasm, depression, stress and cynicism are more by
way of attitudes we can choose to adopt. In the
next two chapters we'll take a look at vision and

relationships, but right now let's briefly explore what I like to call the 'gratitude attitude' and the 'forgiveness factor'.

The Gratitude Attitude

Somebody said that no gift is truly ours until we've thanked the giver. 'Thank you' is something that we are taught as children but that we often forget as adults. To express gratitude in all areas, even the most mundane, is life affirming. How sad it is to hear a person say that they don't expect a thank you. Perhaps there is a person who has become so acclimatised to ingratitude that they now feel unable to receive it. Indeed, there are those who protest at praise and decline to even receive the thanks that are offered. Gratitude is a precious gift that is not diminished in those who give it, no matter how liberally.

It is an undeniable fact of life that grateful people are always happy, even when they have nothing and that ungrateful people are always unhappy, even when they have everything.

Once we have perceived this truth and appropriated its implications, it will make a vast difference to our lives. Mrs Nguyen Thi An had learned the secret. The development of the 'gratitude attitude' will undoubtedly go a long way to enhancing in us a more positive lifestyle. Saint Paul was able to write: *'I have learned to be content whatever the circumstances'* (Philippians 4:11). He knew what it was to be hungry and afraid, to be persecuted or in despair. His attitude and response was something he had to learn. In almost every one of his letters he expressed his thankfulness to God and to his friends. I think it was the fact that he had *learned* this redemptive attitude that made him an apostle.

I'm still very much a disciple!

Be joyful always; pray continually; give thanks in all circumstances, for this is God's will for you in Christ Jesus.

(1 Thessalonians 5:16–18)

No one suggested it would be easy to do these things but it appears, from the verse above, that this is God's will for us. Trying to fashion our lives in accordance with the Maker's instructions seems to me the best safeguard for a good life. However, there is something that is even harder to practise than joy or gratitude.

The Forgiveness Factor

Coupled with the gratitude attitude and, quite possibly springing out of it, is the forgiveness factor. Forgiveness is simply the single most powerful force upon the earth for it is the most dynamic out-working of love. When it is real it is one of the hardest and most costly things to give or to receive. It is much misunderstood and often handled lightly or carelessly. People who push past you in a queue or who step on your toes in the Underground are quick to say 'Sorry' or 'Excuse me', but it means little. I hear people who are annoyed with me say 'Sooo reee!' and, of course, it means just the opposite. But, equally disturbing is the response, 'That's OK' or 'It's all right', when we apologise to someone. And I do so hate the rather patronising 'Apology accepted'. It certainly is not 'OK' or 'all right' or the apology would not have been needed in the first place. If we are sincerely asked for forgiveness we should offer it graciously. To do otherwise is to demean the one who asks.

The world we live in today can be a very unforgiving place. One business stated: 'To err is human . . . to forgive is not company policy.' We might think of the bitterness and unforgiveness that lies at the heart of conflicts in places like the Middle East, Northern Ireland and the former Yugoslavia. Other areas may come to mind but so too will individuals we know. There will be the former work colleagues who are no longer talking to each other, the daughter estranged from her father, the church fellowship splitting up, the marriage that has fallen apart. And all for the want of forgiveness.

You may consider me naïve to put so many breakdowns at the door of unforgiveness. Well, I'm only a clown, but it seems to me that rather than 'forgive and forget', too many of us forget to forgive. When a friend makes a mistake we shouldn't rub it in we should rub it out! The problem is – we don't. We brood on the shortcomings of others. We say we forgive but we bring it up again at times of stress. One of the silliest slogans I've ever heard is 'Love means never having to say you're sorry'. It's ideas like that that have got us into such a mess. Being willing to say 'sorry' is exactly what love is all about! Giving and forgiving are the heartbeat of any strong relationship.

Withholding forgiveness can lead to spiritual, emotional and even physical breakdown. When the forgiveness can be truly given or received, it is not unusual for physical healing and release to take place. In the belief that forgiveness brings healing and reconciliation, a group of Christians undertook

a pilgrimage to the Middle East in 1998, to ask forgiveness of the Arabs for the atrocities inflicted by
Christians during the Crusades. It was the same
desire for healing that led Jill Saward to forgive the
gang that raped her and beat up her father, the
Revd. Michael Saward. We can choose to forgive,
be it ever so hard; but if we do so we draw the poi-
son from the wound and remove the dagger from
our hearts. The deeply moving short story, *Tilly* by
Frank Peretti, deals with one of the toughest areas
of unresolved hurt and the failure to forgive.[3] In
this case, it is perhaps the worst kind: failure to forgive yourself. I won't spoil the tale by being more
specific, but I defy you to read it without shedding
a tear or learning a valuable lesson about forgiveness.

No one said forgiveness was easy. It took Jesus
to a cross because only forgiveness was powerful
enough to hold him up there. Whenever I see the
image of Jesus on a church window or crucifix or
read those heart stopping words in Luke's Gospel
– 'Father, forgive them' – then I remember that forgiveness is at the very centre of the Christian faith.
It has the power to imprison or to set free and,
should we choose to release it or withhold it, we
determine which it is to be. Thin skinned as we are,
we fear the pain of rejection and that inhibits us.

'Forgiveness is the perfume the trampled flower
casts upon the heel that crushed it.' It is quotes like
this one that make us realise how costly forgiveness is and, equally, how valuable. When we pray
'Forgive us our trespasses, as we forgive those who
trespass against us', do we ever pause to think
what a good thing it is that God doesn't answer
that prayer? If God truly forgave us 'as' (Gk. *kai*

gar), or in the same way that we forgive others, all of us would be in a right mess! Unforgiveness begins when we assert our rights, when we start to think the world owes us a living. It's all too easy to fail to recognise our own faults or be willing to change. Estrangement leads to resentment and we choose to be cool and indifferent to others: to ignore them, snub them, and gossip about them. Attitudes like this can be as deadly as murder. Jesus' teaching on the subject in Matthew chapter 5 verses 21 to 26, is very uncompromising. Anger and bitter speech that spring from unforgiveness are roundly condemned. Unforgiveness will severely hinder our relationship with God and inhibit any offering we might make him.

Almost the first story in the Bible shows how easily unforgiveness and resentment can lead to murder. Cain's cynical cry echoes down the centuries in the ears of all that choose not to forgive and forget: 'Am I my brother's keeper?' The mark God put on Cain meant that nobody could kill him. The fantasy writer Karl Edward Wagner draws on this for inspiration with his anti-hero, Kane, the mystic swordsman, a man who is doomed to wander eternity seeking to put right what first he made wrong and perhaps to find forgiveness. Adam's first-born and his fate is a reminder to all that, if not from divine prompting, then at least from a realisation of shared humanity, we must choose to forgive. Perhaps the response from a grieving God to that terrible first question might have been: 'No, but you *are* your brother's brother!'

Strange isn't it that this huge area of our lives, by far the biggest of the three looked at in this book, should be such a contradictory phenomenon? We can't live *without* work and, for many it seems, you can't live *with* it. No wonder that God told Adam, after he'd made his disastrous choice, that he would only eat the fruit of the earth through painful toil and by the sweat of his brow! Gratitude and Forgiveness are certainly factors that can make the toil less painful. Let us take a look at some of the ways in which Vision and Relationship can mop up some of the sweat.

FIFTH PUFF:
IMPROVING YOUR AIM

When good Bishop Denis laid hands on me at Southwell Minster in June of 1980 it wasn't because I'd been caught filching the Communion wine. I was being ordained and I heard spoken over me both then and a year later the words: 'Send down O Lord, your Holy Spirit upon this your servant John for the office and work of a deacon/priest in the church of God.' Even then I don't think I was under any illusions about what God had called me to and although my views, prejudices and expectations have mellowed and matured somewhat over the years I know in every fibre of my being that I have a vital ministry to exercise. God has called me to 'make disciples', to 'equip the saints for ministry', to be a leader under the Good Shepherd in his church. And when my area pastor, Bishop Laurie, laid hands on me in St Margaret's, Stanford-le-Hope and said: 'Receive this cure of souls . . .' I knew what I had to do. Along with others I began making plans to see that souls got cured!

A Goal to Aim For
The point I'm trying to make is that we need a purpose, a goal for which to aim. If we don't discover

this we're lost. I was under no illusions when I was ordained; I was under a vision! The book of Proverbs (chapter 29 verse 18) tells us that 'where there is no vision, the people perish', AV (or 'cast off restraint', NIV). Without vision we die; with vision we are literally restrained, 'tied in' to a God-given direction. Whatever 'god' we put our trust in, if we have no purpose for our lives our work will be meaningless, squalid and ineffectual.

Let me speak as a parish priest for a moment: one of those 'at the coalface'. I love my work and I love the people I am privileged to serve, even (no, *especially*) the Mothers' Union. I can honestly say, and don't forget that clowns are truthspeakers, that it is an enormous joy to be a vicar. I've often thought why this might be. Is it because I have a loving congregation, supportive churchwardens and an understanding church council? This is true but it's not the reason. Is it because my bishop and archdeacon encourage me? (If they're reading this, I'm not looking for promotion, honest!) This is true but it's not the reason. Is it because my wife and children love me even though I'm a vicar? This is particularly true but it's not the reason.

There are lots of reasons why I might be so happy in my work but after much scratching of my clown brain I've come to the conclusion that it is simply because I'm in the place God wants me to be, following the vision and purpose he's given me. Bob Gass writes:

> . . . your destiny fulfilled is the only thing you'll want to face God with. He won't say 'well done' over the money you've made or the reputation you've built. He'll only say it because you found and fulfilled his purpose.[1]

I really believe that if the miserable church folk I was writing about earlier found and followed the purpose God made them for, then they'd be a whole lot happier and their churches would be much nicer places to be. I think the same is true for the cynical vicars I sometimes bump into. I'm sure the same is true for the church as a whole. The Lord God designed each one of us to worship him. Augustine recognised this in his much quoted '. . . our hearts are restless until they find their rest in you'. The Westminster Confession states: 'The chief end of man is to worship God and enjoy him for ever.' The Bible says we should love God with all our heart, soul and strength (Deuteronomy 6) and Jesus commands us in Matthew 28 to 'make disciples of all nations' (v 19).

A lot of congregations (and not just in the Church of England) are going nowhere because they're aiming nowhere. Passionless and purposeless they meet week by week, struggling to pay the bills necessary to keep the building standing and the services ticking over. What's the point in that?

Goal Setting for Churches

In the last twenty to thirty years goal setting and mission statements have become a great feature of business and commerce. Quality Assurance and Total Quality Management are some of the phrases bandied about the office and boardroom. But the Bible has understood the value of aims and goals for thousands of years. It's only recently the church has begun to catch on.

In the early 1990s a church in Illinois, USA, called Willow Creek Community Church, came sharply into focus with its remarkable growth rate.

The phrases 'seeker friendly' and 'seeker sensitive' began to be a regular part of church growth parlance. What pastor Bill Hybels and his team had begun to do was to clearly state their vision and aims and to consequently implement a radical programme designed to accomplish them. The church's vision, simply stated, was 'to turn irreligious people into totally devoted followers of Jesus Christ'. In a relatively short space of time Willow Creek grew from a handful of believers to over 15,000 people.

Happily, Willow Creek is not unique in the Christian Church but it does serve to illustrate that having clear aims and goals does help to encourage growth. Even more important, purpose promotes positive outlook and saves us from atrophy and decay.

Sodalities and Modalities

For some years church growth specialists have recognised the difference between the 'sodal' and the 'modal' approach; in other words, the task-orientated church and the people-orientated church. At the All-Asia Mission Consultation in Seoul, Korea at the end of 1973, Ralph Winter delivered an address that had far-reaching implications not only for church growth, but also for many other areas of community life. The paper was subsequently published under the title: 'The Two Structures of God's Redemptive Mission'. The talk dealt mainly with sodal development and modal development: being task-orientated or being people-orientated.

As any community develops and grows it will tend to be orientated either towards its members or towards its perceived goals and objectives. For example, the classic modality is any town or village. I wonder what effect it would have on your local councillor to be told, 'This area is a classic modality'? Membership requirements are very low: you only have to live there to be a part of it. Most of life in this community is geared to the utilitarian 'greatest good for the greatest number' approach. Most communities like this have no specific corporate goals or 'mission'. The police force (or fire brigade) that serves this community however, is a classic example of a sodality. Membership requirements are very high – you will need to pass a set of demanding examinations and achieve a certain standard if you wish to be accepted. Failure to reach this standard will mean dismissal. The police force and the fire brigade (and indeed many other similar organisations) have clearly defined goals that they expect to achieve. They are task-orientated groups and they could operate in no other way. It is not unusual to see a sodal organisation working on behalf of a modal organisation.

The principles also apply in church life. Groups of Christians who set out with a clearly defined set of goals to which all are expected to adhere are task-orientated. In this category we usually find cults, parachurch movements and missionary organisations. Christian groups that set out to be more pastoral, hesitating to make decisions without the full mandate of the membership are people orientated. Here we find most well established congregations like your own local church and the majority of denominations. The dear old C. of E. is probably the greatest modality in existence!

There are benefits and pitfalls to both approaches and it is very valuable to assess each. The sodal

and modal types are also found in the Bible. In Acts
15, we read of a 'sharp disagreement' between Paul
and Barnabas, regarding the disciple, John Mark.
Paul, clearly a strongly task-orientated missionary,
feels that John Mark will not help them to achieve
their goals since his past performance had shown
him to be unreliable. Barnabas (whose name means
'son of encouragement') is obviously a people-orientated pastor who believes leaving the young
man behind will damage his confidence and possibly set back his faith. Modal individuals and sodal
individuals do tend to clash since their motivation
is so different. However, an objective study of both
can lead to the establishment of strong teamwork.
Modal communities can show us the tremendous
value of strong relationships. When these are in
place the work environment can become more like
a home than a prison. We will look at this in a later
chapter. The sodal approach can teach us that, in
both the secular and the sacred, sound objectives
can lead to satisfying work and ministry.

More and more churches are beginning to wake
up to the value of goal-setting and quite a number
now have clearly stated vision and mission statements. For the record, our mission statement is '*to
be a growing church in which we can deepen our relationship with God and one other*'. The outworking of
this is in six key areas: Glorifying the Lord,
Releasing the Church, Outreach to the World,
Warfare with the enemy, Training the Disciple and
Healing the Community. The more observant
among you will have noticed that the initial letters
of those six areas spell the word 'Growth', which is
our fundamental aim.

Far be it from me to suggest that St Margaret's

has got it all together. We're struggling along and trying hard. And I'm far from being the perfect vicar – very far in fact. But like most clowns I know that God loves a cheerful failure. And my one big advantage is that I'm where God wants me and he believes in me. That, as I've said, is the supreme reason I'm happy in my work.

When I stand at the Holy Table each Sunday my eyes fill with tears as I say to my congregation, 'Let us give thanks to the Lord our God' and they reply, 'It is right to give him thanks and praise.' 'It's not only right,' I tell them, 'it's our *duty* and our *joy*.'

Vision and purpose in our work and walk with God, loving him and doing his will, is not just a responsibility, it's an incredible joy!

On the other hand . . . if you aim at nothing . . . you're sure to hit it.

SIXTH PUFF:
PASSION RESTORED AND WORK REDEEMED

We've looked at the problems in the world of work, the drive that pushes us to achieve and the demanding sense of 'have to' that we all grapple with. We've explored the rapidly expanding world of choice and information and the great pressure they put upon us. We've seen that the increase of labour-saving devices has complicated rather than simplified our lives, and thrust us into more work. Work can become a many-headed monster that seeks constantly to devour us, or an idol that we are forced to worship and appease. Yet, we've also seen that work is a good and necessary part of our lives and that it can bring much satisfaction. In its proper place and focus, work is part of what we need to do in society; the contribution we make in the lives we lead.

Work does not authenticate us – we are what we are, not what we do – yet work is a precious gift and everyone should have the right to engage in it without fear or favour. Work is much more than paid employment: it is a task that moves towards a goal. For work to take its place alongside rest and play it must enable us and encourage us. It must have purpose.

Gratitude, forgiveness and vision are more than attitudes to adopt; they are lifestyles in which we can choose to live. In this last section, we will look at the places, times and, most of all, relationships, that enable us and that can restore our passion and enthusiasm.

Enthusiasm and Passion

I am a clown in holy orders, a sacred fool, as I've already told you. I am also a high 'I'. Now you probably won't have a clue what I'm on about unless you've been inducted into the mysteries of Myers Briggs and/or the 'DISC' system. These are clever programmes, usually involving multiple choice questions that seek to determine your personality profile. In these days of increasing political correctness, more and more organisations are using them to determine suitability for a particular job. They don't always get it right, of course. Here's one I picked up the other day:

JORDAN MANAGEMENT CONSULTANTS
397 Jericho Road Jerusalem 91-000 Israel

Jesus, Son of Joseph
Woodcrafter's Carpenter Shop
Nazareth

Thank you for submitting the resumés of the twelve men you have selected for management positions in your new organisation. All of them have taken our battery of tests and we have run the results through our computer. We have arranged for each to have personal interviews with our psychologists and vocational aptitude consultants. The complete profile on each is included for your careful study.

It is our staff's opinion that most of your staff nomi-

nees are lacking in background, education and vocational aptitude for the type of work you are undertaking. They do not demonstrate a team concept. We would recommend that you search for persons of experience in managerial ability and proven capability.

Simon Peter is emotionally unstable and given to an offensive temper. Andrew has absolutely no qualities of leadership. Brothers James and John, the sons of Zebedee, place personal interest above company loyalty. Frankly they are 'Mamma's boys'. Thomas demonstrates a questioning attitude that would tend to undermine morale. We feel that it is our duty to tell you that Matthew has been blacklisted by our Greater Jerusalem Business Bureau. James, the son of Alphaeus, and Thaddaeus have definite leanings towards the radical and register high on the manic depressive scale.

One of the candidates does, however, show great potential. He is a man of ability and resourcefulness, meets people well, and has a keen business mind. He is highly motivated as well as ambitious and responsible. We recommend Judas Iscariot as your controller and right-hand man.

All other profiles are self-explanatory.

We wish you every success in your new venture.

I did my personality profile several years ago as part of a team in another parish. The answers to my questions determined me as a high 'I' or 'influencing' kind of person. The top word that apparently summed me up was 'enthusiastic'. I remember the other members of the team, on learning this, saying (very tongue-in-cheek), 'No! . . . Really?'

OK, I'll admit it; I'm an enthusiast. If I'm keen on something I rave about it, from pineapple and anchovy pizza and mint chocolate chip ice cream to the latest *Star Trek: Voyager* video; from the growth of the church in Korea to my son's latest cartoon or daughter's recent story. I'm passionate and I don't care who knows.

I'm all for enthusiasm! The Christian author and sociologist, Tony Campolo, writes: '*I feel, therefore, I am.*' I like that! In one of his latest books, *Carpe Diem*,[1] Professor Campolo bemoans the loss of passion in so many people. He writes of the workers who live their lives in 'quiet desperation' who, on Monday, are already counting the hours until the end of the week; the kids whose unfeeling manners are summed up in the word 'cool'. Like Tony Campolo, I don't want to be cool; I want to be hot! The preacher, John Wesley, wrote, 'Let a man of God get on fire and people will come to watch him burn.'

I can't understand this denigration of emotion and passion. Friends and family often get embarrassed when I greet bus drivers or chat cheerily with waiters and checkout girls. It's the clown in me, I suppose. Most of all, I am appalled by the lack of passion in worship. When we declare our praises to the living God we should be prepared to be like a football crowd, wildly cheering their team's latest goal. Instead, we're more like a conservative British test match group, politely applauding the Almighty and saying quietly, 'Jolly well done.' If a friend we loved very much had terminal cancer with only weeks to live and someone unexpectedly discovered a complete miracle cure, I doubt even the most restrained of us would say, 'Jolly well done.'

There are certainly times when worship should be intense and ecstatic, full of emotion and passion;

sometimes quiet and reflective, sometimes loud and exuberant, but always, always, *with feeling*.

Passion is an interesting concept to explore, particularly in the field of work. In Matthew 9 verse 36 we read that when Jesus 'saw the crowds, he had compassion on them, because they were harassed and helpless, like sheep without a shepherd'. Compassion literally means 'with feeling' and it was this attitude of enthusiastic love that motivated Jesus' work and prompted his plea to the disciples to ask God (the Lord of the harvest) to send more 'workers'. I am convinced that more compassion would result not only in fuller and friendlier churches but also fuller and friendlier 'workers', willing and able to work in the 'harvest field'.

Spiritual Passion

But where is this spiritual passion to be obtained? It cannot simply be manufactured. In his excellent book, *Restoring your Spiritual Passion*, Gordon MacDonald paints the picture of a family driving along a dusty rural Canadian road looking for a place to spend the night. The hour is late, they've been travelling a long time but there seems to be no signs indicating direction or distance and the route is not marked on their map. The family is tired and irritable, their former zeal has utterly abated and what previously had been exciting and enjoyable has now become complete drudgery. I can understand that, I remember being there myself and I can see the parallel with many lives where dryness, tiredness and emptiness have entered into our very souls. Spiritual passion is dead.

Gordon MacDonald gives a number of superb illustrations and suggestions as to how we might

restore our passion and three particularly have
stayed in my mind. They relate to the Map of our
lives, the Diary of our lives and the Address Book
of our lives or, as Gordon MacDonald puts it: 'Safe
Places', 'Still Times' and 'Special Friends'. The out-
working of these three areas has had such a profound effect upon my life and work that I wanted
to take just a few lines to share it with you. Most of
the ideas are based firmly on the insights gleaned
from *Restoring your Spiritual Passion*.[2]

Sanctuaries

One of my favourite black and white films from the
past is *The Hunchback of Notre Dame* with Charles
Laughton in the title role. I well remember the
scene where the hunchback rescues the gypsy
Esmeralda from the soldiers and, as he swings back
with her into the tower, cries, 'Sanctuary!
Sanctuary!' Sanctuaries are safe places where we
can find peace, rest and restoration. The psalmist
writes: 'You are my hiding place; you will protect
me from trouble and surround me with songs of
deliverance' (Psalm 32:7).

Safe places can be found anywhere but rightly
recognised they restore spiritual passion. They
might be in a church or retreat house, a study or
office, the corner of a bedroom, a holiday destination, a clearing in a wood. They will usually be
cosy, familiar and safe. Even now when my children have nightmares or face spiders (well,
Hannah anyway), their safe place is snug in Mum
and Dad's bed (with Mum and Dad, of course).

In the Bible we find many examples of safe
places and we can understand the anger of Jesus
when he found one of the most important (the tem-

ple) desecrated. In 2 Samuel 16 the safe place for David is Bahurim where, we read, 'he refreshed himself'. In Joshua 4 before the walls of Jericho, Gilgal becomes a safe place as the children of Israel remember God's past blessings. In the Cave of Adullam in 1 Samuel 22 the distressed and discontented find refuge and new confidence and the manic depressive Elijah finds a safe place on Mount Horeb (1 Kings 19) where God's 'gentle whisper' gives him new purpose and direction.

Safe places are places of refreshment, remembrance, refuge and redirection. When our spiritual passion is ebbing, our work has become meaningless and our life is dry, a stay in the safe place is called for. It won't necessarily be the most obvious place: for Shadrach, Meshach and Abednego it was a fiery furnace and for the first martyr, Stephen it was (incredibly) the place of his death. He had discovered what Paul later affirmed in Colossians 3 verse 3: 'For you died, and your life is now hidden with Christ in God.'

In June 1980 I was travelling as a passenger in a car to my ordination in Nottingham when, on a sharp bend, the vehicle turned over. Petrol squirted out of the tank; we should have exploded but we didn't. My window smashed inward showering glass all over me; I should have been cut but I wasn't. Our vehicle lay helpless in the middle of a busy road; we should have been struck by another car but we weren't. We emerged unscathed; the car was a write off. Somehow, a place of great danger had become a safe place. Later that day I received a letter from overseas and in it were words from Psalm 91, David's great song of protection.

'Because he loves me,' says the LORD, 'I will
     rescue him;
     I will protect him, for he acknowledges
     my name.
He will call upon me, and I will answer him;
     I will be with him in trouble, I will
     deliver him and honour him.
With long life will I satisfy him
     and show him my salvation.'
                              (Psalm 91:14–16)

A safe place is somewhere to discover who God is.

Sabbath Moments

A still time is a Sabbath moment. I write extensive-
ly about this in the last section of the book. Stillness
is absolutely vital for restoring spiritual passion. It
is often (though not always) in the safe place that
we have the still time. Elijah's still time was listening to the Lord's still small voice. In Psalm 46, in
the midst of war, earthquake and upheaval we
read, 'Be still and know that I am God.' A still time
is a time that is different, a time that is 'other', apart
from the rest of our week: a time to observe and to
evaluate. The still time is not just a day in the week
or a period of the year. It is a life principle that will
lay bedrock in our soul and restore our passion.
Failure to appreciate the value of still times and the
need to practise the habit of 'Sabbath moments' is
a major contributory factor in the growth of work
as a monster rather than a friend. We need to fill
our spiritual diaries with still times. Still times are
moments for discovering what God wants.

Aaron and Hur

Special friends remind us of the enduring value of personal relationships. In Exodus 17 we read of Joshua leading the Israelites against the Amalekites at Rephidim. As they fought the ancient Moses stood on a nearby hill. As he raised his arms Joshua's army prevailed; when they were lowered the Amalekites triumphed. As Moses became weary he sat on a rock and his friends, Aaron and Hur, held up his arms. These special friends enabled Moses to ensure Joshua and the Israelites won the day. It has been my privilege to have an Aaron and Hur on my team at Stanford-le-Hope in my churchwardens. Kim and I have also discovered the value of special friends in a whole variety of other ways, not least in our 'Prayer Shield', a group of friends from all over the country (and abroad) who pray regularly for us and our children. One of our Shield had a 'picture' of Kim and I walking along a road. There were many obstacles in the way and a number of potholes to avoid. As we progressed a number of people were in front of us removing the obstacles and pointing out the potholes so we could move forward unhindered. It was a prophecy of what our Prayer Shield would do for us and it is a picture of the value of relationships.

In *Restoring Your Spiritual Passion*, Gordon MacDonald gives examples of the varieties of special friends: the Sponsor, the Affirmer, the Rebuker, the Intercessor, the Partner and the Pastor. Special friends will have many of these qualities and again, we find plenty of examples of them in the Bible. Special friends can be of enormous value, especially in the workplace or when there is a task that

needs to be completed. Gordon MacDonald quotes
Joseph Heller in giving an example of the situation
that all too often occurs in an office.

> Often, I protect and defend [Jack Green] when
> he is late or forgetful with work of his own, and
> I frequently give him credit for good work from
> my department that he does not deserve. But I
> never tell him that I do this; and I never let him
> know when I hear anything favourable about
> him. I enjoy seeing Green apprehensive. I'm
> pleased he distrusts me (it does wonders for my
> self-esteem), and I do no more than necessary to
> reassure him.
>
> And I am the best friend he has here.[3]

The 'sting' is in the tail, isn't it? Even our so-called
friends are not that friendly or supportive and, as
for helping us when we're in trouble! A friend in
need . . . is a pain in the neck, as the prodigal son
quickly discovered when his money ran out.

Finding ourselves without special friends or any
kind of meaningful relationships can be very draining and destructive, particularly in our place of
work. My experiences in some churches and my
wife's in a variety of offices yield examples where
enormous strain results from wondering whether
those who are supposed to be for you are actually
against you. Petty competition, gossip and unwillingness to work together can lead to stress and
fatigue. Gordon MacDonald gives the example of a
tandem where the front cyclist is peddling strenu-
ously whilst the second and third sit back and
admire the view. Of course, the situation may be
even worse if two and three are actively trying to

peddle in another direction!

Special friends encourage you; they observe what you are doing and attach value to it. If they are believers they will almost certainly pray for you. They will rejoice when you succeed and weep when you fail.

Special Friends at Play

One remarkable thing I've noticed about children is their ready ability to make friends. They argue and squabble just as readily as adults but they are often quick to make up and forget what took place before. My daughter comes home from school with a look that would sour milk to tell me she's 'broken up' with so-and-so. Apparently she did this, that and the other and they called each other names and that is the end of their friendship. From the description she gives me, it sounds like World War Three broke out at the school and there's going to be no amnesty. The next day Hannah comes home with a bright smile and her ex-friend on her arm. 'I thought you two weren't talking,' I venture naively. 'Oh, no,' say Hannah and her friend, 'that was *yesterday*!'

Would that adults found it as easy to forgive and forget! If only our relationships could have a little more enduring quality about them. It is often in play that we learn the values of friendship that we quickly miss when we are at work. The people we play with, as adults or as children, are the people we like: the ones we get on with. We might think of our golfing partner, the football team we are a part of or the little group that joins us on Friday night for bridge. Very often, the friends who play with us last for a lifetime and are drawn closely into our family circle.

Our friends are people we depend on. They will be there to share in special family occasions like birthdays and weddings and they will support us through the sad times of sickness and bereavement.

Good relationships restore our spiritual passion. True relationship is the foundation of positive life enhancement and will be expressed through gratitude, laughter, encouragement and forgiveness. Our church mission statement contains the word 'relationship' at its heart because it is only on this basis that any community of people, be they churches, businesses or marriages, can hope to prosper and grow.

Special friends are people who enable you to do God's will.

In the film *Beaches* the characters played by Bette Midler and Barbara Hearshey are a classic example of special friends. Childhood companions, they grow up together and entwine their lives. At the end of the film, when one dies, the other adopts her daughter. The poignant song that closes the film sums up the essential qualities of a special friend.

Don't you know that you're my hero?
You're everything I long to be.
You lift me higher than an eagle.
You are the wind beneath my wings.[4]

It is the special friends, the still times and the safe places that restore our spiritual passion when the candle of our enthusiasm is flickering out. Simon Peter discovered this shortly after the resurrection. In John 21 we read of him telling his friends, 'I'm going fishing.' Even though Jesus was alive Peter couldn't erase the memory of his betrayal. Deep inside him there was emptiness and he must have felt his relationship with Jesus could never be restored. But Peter could find no solace or meaning, even in his familiar work, and the night passed without fish and without hope.

I've been in that place of emptiness and despair and I expect you have too. The mystics sometimes refer to it as 'the long dark night of the soul'. But as the disciples' boat drifts listlessly towards shore a voice rings out through the early morning mists . . . and everything changes! When Jesus speaks into our lives emptiness is filled and passion restored. The disciples' nets are filled with fish and in moments Peter is on the beach taking breakfast with his Special Friend. And in that Safe Place, Jesus and Peter take a Still Time to walk along the beach together. Words of encouragement, correction, instruction and direction reinstate Peter's livelihood and ministry. Passion is restored.

I'm more grateful than I can say for safe places to go and still times to spend and special friends to share them with. And whatever the personality profiles may say the influence of these upon my life is immeasurable.

Attitude is everything. We are what we are but, by the grace of God, we can choose what we will be. Restored passion, perpetual thankfulness, sacrificial forgiveness, lasting relationships: these are the beacons that shine in the world of work, that environment that can sometimes be so dark and cold. They let the air out of the balloon for a moment, allowing us to transform something that was full of pressure and torsion into a thing of rare

beauty and delight. Sometimes it is only a small
change that is needed to transform the whole attitude and perspective: a twist here, a turn there.
Passion is restored and work, that strange and
complex beast, is redeemed.

I often think of those runners from *Chariots of
Fire*, pounding through the surf to the haunting
strains of *Vangelis*: working, yes, striving to
achieve, certainly, but doing it with the passion and
enthusiasm that made them champions. And I
think of Paul's words:

> But one thing I do: Forgetting what is behind
> and straining towards what is ahead, I press on
> towards the goal to win the prize for which God
> has called me heavenwards in Christ Jesus.
>
> (Philippians 3:13–14)

One thing I ask
(Psalm 27)

Play

What we like to do

'We don't stop playing because we grow old; we grow old because we stop playing.'
George Bernard Shaw

'I tell you the truth, unless you change and become like little children, you will never enter the kingdom of heaven.'
Jesus (Matthew 18:3)

FIRST TWIST:
SEND IN THE CLOWNS

When Francis of Assisi sent his followers out he gave them this simple message: '*Preach the gospel to everyone; use words if you have to.*'

St Francis was sometimes referred to as God's Fool and this is the inspiration behind my clown character 'Gof', God's Own Fool. Gof and John have a lot in common, besides being the same person, of course. There are a good many things that Gof can do that John can't, and there are certainly things that John can do that Gof can't (although Gof would probably disagree with me on that one).

Gof is (at the moment) a Whiteface clown whose character and qualities have been developing over the past fourteen years. He's a dab hand at balloon modelling and fancies himself as a bit of an amateur magician but his best quality is interacting with people (especially children), and making them feel good about themselves. He tends to get very confused and causes a lot of chaos to people around him but his heart's in the right place – right out there on his sleeve! When Gof's around things do tend to get turned upside down and inside out but it all generally works out in the end. At least everyone has lots of fun.

Clowns

Clowns, fools and jesters have been around for thousands of years, of course. There are even records of them in Ancient Egypt. The word 'clown' comes from the old English for 'clod', or lump of earth. These were the village idiots, the 'rude mechanicals' of Shakespeare's *Midsummer Night's Dream*. And there's me thinking they were 'rude' because one of them was called Bottom!

In medieval times clowns were found in court in the shape of jesters and these characters form a strong theme through many of Shakespeare's plays. In *King Lear*, the Fool is given many of the wisest lines to utter.

Fool: If a man's brains were in's heels, were't not in danger of kibes?

Lear: Ay, boy.

Fool: Then, I prithee, be merry; thy wit shall ne'er go slip-shod.

Deep stuff, eh? Well, I'm sure the Bard had them rolling in the aisles at the Globe with that one!

It was the job of the court jester to divert the king from the more serious business of governing the land by telling jokes and performing tricks to amuse him. The jokes would sometimes be a little 'near the knuckle' as the fool sought to make the monarch see truth and reality through humour. Here the jester walked a precarious tightrope for a line too 'near the knuckle' would mean him losing his job . . . and probably his head as well! To be a clown is often to take enormous risks. We certainly get ridiculed and laughed at and we sometimes get hurt as well.

In the last two hundred years we have seen the development of clowns through theatre and circus. Pierrot, Harlequin and Columbine and Grimaldi and Coco are names we readily associate with different clowns. In the past seventy years, particularly through the rise of the circus, clowns have fallen into three main characters: the Whiteface, the Auguste and the Hobo or Tramp Clown, the latter being made famous in America, particularly by Red Skelton.

Clowns are usually recognisable by their make-up and outrageous colourful clothing. The Tramp or Hobo Clown will usually wear dark and tatty clothes and have a sad and mournful face. If there's a wrong way of doing things he usually does it and he has a tendency to get put on by others. He is far from miserable however and has the wonderful gift of evoking sympathy in others. The Auguste we generally associate with the circus. Nicolai Poliakoff, otherwise known as Coco the Clown, is probably the most famous. The Auguste is the one with the huge misshapen jacket and the baggy trousers. He is the character for whom the German word 'klutz' must have been invented. The Whiteface, as his name suggests, has predominantly white makeup and is usually dressed quite smartly. He is the foil for the Auguste and tries to boss them about. Inevitably, his pomposity is punctured and he is made to look foolish. Nowadays, the distinctions between the different kinds of clowns have become quite blurred and they don't always act true to form. For instance, Gof is really a Whiteface but he doesn't act like one. (Mind you, he was *supposed* to be a silent clown too!)

A clown's make-up can have great significance,

particularly for those who are Christians. Mine takes about an hour to put on and I try to do it in complete silence as a kind of meditation, to remind me for whom I'm doing it. The white is a symbol of death and it reminds me of the verses that tell us of the need to die to ourselves. On top of the white are placed the bright colours of resurrection and new life, and this reminds me that I have a new outlook and a new attitude because God's Spirit now lives in me. The prop that most epitomises the clown is the big red nose. Plastic, foam or greasepaint; it shows us that here is a fool who will invite ridicule and laughter. The red nose is evocative of the inebriate, someone who is not fully in control of themselves. It also reminds us of someone who has been thumped or who has a bad cold, an echo of the suffering that can hide behind the smile. Even before they speak, clowns can be a parable, a walking picture of the message they are called to convey.

Not all clowns wear red noses and baggy trousers. Some of the best known are the giants of the silent screen: Chaplin, Keaton, Laurel and Hardy. They are perhaps more easy to recognise as clowns because their humour, being silent, was so visual, although all of them transferred their talent to the 'talkies', with varying degrees of success. The Music Hall brought many clowns into the public eye and a new genre of entertainment developed. Nowadays, we have a whole host of comedians, not all of whom we might classify as clowns. Everyone will have his or her particular favourites so I won't single out anyone in particular.

Clowning is particularly popular in North America and each year a number of 'Clown Camps' are run to assist clowns in their character and performance skills. Mostly, we just go to have fun together. Clowns in the US and Canada are formed into local groups called 'Alleys', presumably taken from the French 'Allez-oop', used in the circus. Clowns are involved in circus skills such as slackrope and tightrope walking, juggling, wobble-board, devil sticks and diabolo as well as balloon modelling, comedy magic, face painting and a whole variety of skits and gags. Clowns perform in schools, hospitals, old people's homes, prisons, clubs and pubs, theatres and on the street. Some of them also work in churches.

Holy Fools

In addition to the foolish Francis of Assisi there have been a variety of clown-like figures in church history. There's a whole list of fools in the Bible, up to and including John the Baptist, whose 'motley' was made of camel hair and whose diet was locusts in honey! The Eastern Orthodox Church has the rare and unusual office of 'salos', a kind of clown/fool/prophet. When Francis took his clothes off and ran naked in the street he was engaged in a kind of prophetic foolishness. According to Jean-Jacques Suurmond, one salos, a monk named Symeon, entered a city dragging a dead dog behind him!

> He entered the women's baths naked, relieved himself in the market-place, forced his way into a room where a woman was sleeping and made as if he were going to take off his garments, and during a church service mounted the pulpit to pelt the congregation with notes.[1]

While the clown's role is to make people laugh, it is

also to make them think. In this way they can behave similarly to the prophets of old. Often the clown will offend or embarrass, although they will never seek intentionally to do this. (Symeon the monk excepted, I suppose!) However, the clown will always provoke a reaction.

Quite a number of clowns today are practising Christians. I say 'practising' because none of us have got it right yet. In 1983, Revd. Roly Bain founded 'Holy Fools', a loose-knit collection of loose nits who wanted to clown around for God. Now Roly, voted International Clown of the Year in 1994, works fool-time, clowning around in schools, churches and synods all over the place. In his first book, *Fools Rush In,* Roly writes,

> Where there are places that angels fear to tread, the clown steps up as the eternal volunteer, saying 'Here am I, send me', for nothing is too fearful or too sacred or too much for him. Clowns are both fools and angels, messengers of God entrusted with the Good News of his Kingdom as well as the care of his children.[2]

It may sound weird to equate clowns with angels but it's not so strange, you know. We are messengers from God, just like Francis and his first disciples. And whether in mime or word, through gag or skit, by humour, suffering and pathos, we communicate the Good News of the kingdom to those we meet.

The world of the clown is often upside down and inside out: very much like the gospel in fact. If you want to be rich then give away all you have; if you want to be great become the slave of all; you'll find true maturity by becoming like a child, and if you want to be wise then embrace foolishness. Further still, we find joy in suffering and new life through death. The world was changed by a bunch of illiterate ragamuffins masquerading as apostles and proclaiming faith in an itinerant Jewish rabbi, executed for treason and sedition. Two thousand years later we're still teaching that you can have a personal relationship with the man who died on a hill outside Jerusalem and our prime symbol is an ancient implement of torture. Daft isn't it . . . and utterly glorious! Do you wonder that Christian clowns love to spread this foolishness?

Jesus the Fool

Of course God's Fool is really the Lord Jesus, whose message, Paul tells us, is a stumbling block to Jews and foolishness to Gentiles. And he continues:

> For the foolishness of God is wiser than man's wisdom, and the weakness of God is stronger than man's strength.

> (1 Corinthians 1:25)

The musical *Godspell* portrays Jesus as a clown. Some may find portrayal of the King of kings and Lord of lords as a fool, to be sacrilegious. This is hardly strange, given the comments made by Paul in his first Corinthian letter. Michael Frost has written a book called *Jesus the Fool*.[3] He paints the picture of a Jesus so unlike the Hollywood image of the bearded superstar with piercing blue eyes. He writes of a Jesus who turns upside down the assumptions and presumptions of his day: a Jesus who, like a court jester, spoke the unspeakable and 'reframed' the perceptions of his contemporaries. He still does it today. Jesus is a Fool, not because he is stupid and senseless. He is a Fool, supremely because, having died a hideous death at the hands of his own creation, he returns to love the very people who crucified him: you and me. As Michael Frost says: 'Not because we deserve him, but because his crazy love for us can do nothing else.'

The theologian and singer, Michael Card, put it this way in his song, *God's Own Fool*:

Seems I've imagined him all of my life,
As the wisest of all of mankind
But if God's holy wisdom was foolish to men,
He must have seemed out of his mind.
Even his family said he was mad
And the priests said, 'A demon's to blame',
But God in the form of this angry young man
Could not have seemed perfectly sane.

We in our foolishness thought we were wise
He played the fool and he opened our eyes.
We in our weakness believed we were strong
He became helpless to show we were wrong.
So we follow God's Own Fool
For only the foolish can tell
Believe the unbelievable,
Come, be a fool as well.

So come live your life for a carpenter's son
For a madman who died for a dream.
Then you'll have the faith his first followers had
And you'll feel the weight of the beam.
So surrender the hunger to say you must know
Have the courage to say, 'I believe.'

For the power of paradox opens your eyes
And blinds those who say they can see.

We in our foolishness thought we were wise
He played the fool and he opened our eyes.
We in our weakness believed we were strong
He became helpless to show we were wrong.
So we follow God's Own Fool
For only the foolish can tell
Believe the unbelievable,
Come, be a fool as well.[4]

The invitation is clear and unmistakable. This gospel is for the weak and lowly and despised. This gospel is for the foolish, for God has chosen to shame the wise. It is for those who are willing and happy to play, joining hands with all God's children in the foolish Circle of the kingdom of heaven.

Clowning in Church

Clowns, as I have said, have been around for a long time, but not everyone understands them. Some people will have nothing to do with them. Cannibals, for example, refuse to eat them because they taste funny! Contrary to common belief, children, particularly the very young, are afraid of clowns. Sometimes they scream, or cry or hide behind the legs of a familiar adult. Gof, I'm pleased to say loves children. He used to go to school with them – in fact, he still does. If he sees any children (or grown-ups) who are frightened or embarrassed, he invariably backs off or waits for them to come to him.

When I run my clown workshops people will come to me and say they had bad experiences with

clowns when they were young. What they need to
get over this, I tell them, is some clownselling. This
usually takes the shape of some fun activities to
help them find themselves. There will be more
about this in the next chapter.

When I start to talk about clowns and clowning
to clergy and church people, many of them raise
their eyebrows and lower their tolerance levels. We
are very inclined to think that faith is a deadly serious matter. It's certainly no laughing matter! When
Gof appeared on the front page of a national
Christian periodical and the editor was thoughtless
enough to reveal that he was also a vicar, letters
were written! Apparently, some people think it is
very disrespectful for a clown and a minister of the
gospel to be the same person. I didn't tell Gof; it
might have upset him. Then again, he'd probably
have a good laugh!

But it's the children, most of all, which the
clown looks for. The eight-year-olds and the
eighty-year-olds! The child that is in all of us. The
child that remembers that first visit to the circus,
that first surprising custard pie and the first time
the baggy-trousered man with the big red nose fell
flat on his back. In his beautiful autobiography,
Coco the Clown writes:

> I cannot retire because I love the smiles of chil-
> dren. Take them away from me and I would not
> last very long. But if I ever have to retire, the
> only way I can see is to open a little sweet shop
> somewhere opposite a school so that children
> will come to me for their shopping. I know I'd
> give away more sweets than I'd sell – but please
> do not take the children away from me.[5]

Clowns help us to play and as such they are good companions on the pilgrimage of faith. They often cause us to stop and think and see things from a different perspective. They enable us to get back on when we've fallen off, readjust our balance and start again. They help us see that, although every silver lining has a cloud, behind the cloud is a bright blue sky and a big yellow sun. They help us to laugh.

So – send in the clowns!

8

SECOND TWIST:
CIRCLES

I've been running Clown Workshops for about six or seven years now, inviting others to join me in discovering the fun and foolishness of playing together. We always begin by forming a circle. This is essential as it reminds us of some important lessons for our lives. First, it is the Circus Ring, where we play and perform and entertain. Second, it is the Arena, where we face suffering and death. Thirdly, it represents the Big Wide World, of which we are all a part.

The Circus Ring is a great place for the clown, for clowns love to draw attention to themselves. They like to play and they love to draw others into that play. The applause of the crowd keeps bringing them back for more and if others are willing to leave the spectators and join in play with the clown then something really worthwhile will have been achieved.

In some ways the Arena is the antithesis of the Circus Ring; in others it is very similar. To enter the circle in full view is to take an incredible risk and sometimes to suffer. Christians are still thrown to lions today and clowns, of all messengers, know what it is to feel pain. In the Arena the clown comes to realise that it is not all non-stop gags and laughter; sometimes we dance on thorns.

The Big Wide World is where we belong. In the circle, we all face one another; that makes us *vulnerable*. But in the circle, as in the world, we are all part of the same group. We are, to coin a phrase, 'all in the same boat' (a fact Jesus' disciples came to realise on more than one occasion). This collegiality brings *encouragement*. The dramatic interplay of vulnerability and encouragement is one of the most important things I attempt to teach in my workshops. The circle illustrates this well. In an inward-facing circle no one can hide; everyone is exposed. It's not like many of our church services where we gaze at the anonymous back of somebody's neck. Settings like that can easily promote isolation and fear.

Vulnerability and Encouragement

Gazing at a group of strangers facing you in a circle can itself be rather alarming at first, until you see that most of them are just as alarmed as you. Multiple thoughts flash through the brain. Why am I here? Whatever possessed me to join this workshop? What are we going to be asked to do next? I feel vulnerable and exposed. I don't even like clowns anyway! Why are we all grinning so idiotically?

For some of us (who can remember) thoughts will go back to that first day at school. I've relived it as my own children have prepared for a new school. How will I cope? How will I know what to do or how will I find my way round an unfamiliar building? And when we arrive, everything seems so different. The teachers are so big and the other children are so noisy. Everything is so strange and alarming. I feel vulnerable and exposed. And then . . . we start to play.

And in the clown workshop circle, feeling vulnerable and exposed again, we start to play. We enjoy ourselves so much, laughing and being silly, that we forget to be afraid. After a while, breathless and a little embarrassed, we are invited (if we wish) to step into the circle, introduce ourselves and share a bit of personal information, preferably of a surprising nature. We start to feel a little nervous and self-conscious again.

My name's John. I'm petrified of sharks . . . Hello, I'm Helen. I started my new diet yesterday . . . I'm Sarah and I like spot-welding . . . Hi, I'm Graham and I became a grandfather for the first time today . . . My name's Beryl. I have arthritis and I think I may have to sit down soon . . . Hello everyone, I'm Brian. I love pancakes. I have a collection of 357 . . . Ummm, I'm Susan and I'm feeling very nervous.

As circle members take the big risk of making themselves even more vulnerable, stepping into the middle and telling everyone some information, from the personal to the mundane, the rest of the group is prompted to respond with encouragement. Everyone is enthusiastically applauded. There are words of appreciation, occasional gasps of wonder, some laughter and much love. We step back from the middle to the edge of the circle feeling a little exhilarated, relieved that we've managed to do it and buoyed up by the support of our new friends. We begin to realise that the others are feeling the same way too; we really are all in the same boat, part of the same circle, clowns in the same ring, suffering in the same arena, all belonging to the same world.

Playing together, we begin to drop some of our barriers and connect with others. Nowhere is this more apparent that in the interplay of vulnerability and encouragement. Someone encourages us to be vulnerable. Our vulnerability elicits encouragement. It really is amazing how a few words of encouragement can produce such a powerful effect. It is like rain or sunshine opening up the tightly closed petals of a flower bud. Hidden talents are exposed. Hitherto unseen qualities come to the fore. A smile plays around the corners of the mouth and laughter is heard. An individual is released! You don't have to be a clown to understand this, but if you are it helps!

There are few things in life more binding than the failure to give encouragement. It is so simple a thing and often so rare. It means taking the trouble to appreciate another individual. The problem is that this does mean making ourselves vulnerable. Saying something nice to another person runs the risk of being spurned. We take the chance that our good words will be trivialised, ridiculed or refused. Even a simple smile could receive a slap in the face, figurative or actual. It is then far easier not to take the risk, not to make ourselves vulnerable. We withhold the kind words, we keep up the barriers and we miss yet another opportunity to connect positively with another human being.

We can all remember being let down in the past. When our naïve good will led us into being laughed at and made fun of. It may have happened at school, it may have happened at home; but somewhere into late childhood we made the decision not to let our guard down so easily the next time. The playful enthusiasm of youth gives way to the cynicism and reserve of so-called 'maturity'. Simon and Garfunkel sang about it so tellingly in their song, *I am a Rock*. Who can say whether the subject of the song would have risked a little vulnerability if they had received a little encouragement? Lack of encouragement and absence of positive input leads inevitably into the downward spiral of negativism and discouragement. We end up behaving like rocks. And we feel no pain. Right?

In his selection of short stories in *On the Anvil*, Max Lucado introduces us to a number of individuals, some fictional, many real, who were destroyed through lack of encouragement. John Hinckley Jr., who attempted to assassinate President Ronald Reagan, might have grown up a different man if his family, his friends, his school or his church, had given him the encouragement we all deserve. Max Lucado writes: 'It is our responsibility to intercept a life like John Hinckley's and fill it with value.'[1]

Emphasising the Positive

True encouragement is a commodity as rare as hen's teeth in some areas. It has been said that there is nothing like a good pat on the back to push the chest out. Everyone needs to feel appreciated. Encouragement goes hand in glove with gratitude. Lack of it inevitably leads to depression and cynicism. There are hordes of gifted, creative people whose talents are largely unrecognised for want of some encouragement earlier in life. Many of them truly believe that anything they might contribute is worthless or would be ridiculed. If a parent, teacher or friend had just taken the opportunity to say: 'Thanks; that was really good, you should do that more often', perhaps it would all have been so different. Some of the greatest household names of stage, screen and television would not be where they are today on the strength of talent alone. It was because someone recognised that talent and *encouraged* it, that they had the growing confidence to succeed. Offices would be nicer environments in which to work, churches would be warmer, marriages would be stronger and families would be happier if the simple work of personal encouragement was allowed to flourish.

The clown circle strives to reverse the direction of the spiral from down to up. Encouragement promotes vulnerability, and vulnerability, in its turn, calls forth encouragement. And you don't have to join one of my workshops to do it (although that would be a good start). Just try a little encouragement and don't be put off by the occasional rebuff or puzzled look. They will be relatively rare. We all tend to remember the negative rather than the positive and the latter is much more common when we take the trouble to look. I usually forget the thirty compliments I receive after a service from my congregation and instead focus on the one 'Hrrmmppp! That service was too long and I didn't like the last hymn!' (Actually, I hardly ever get told that nowadays but the point is valid.) I once held up a piece of paper with a small black dot in the centre and asked the congregation what they could see. Most people saw the spot; hardly anyone saw the huge white expanse of paper.

So don't worry about the tiny amount of criticism you'll receive when you start encouraging people. Focus on the positive and the wonderful response to your small input will encourage you as well. The circle will go round and round as vulnerability leads to encouragement and back again. The Circus Ring for the entertainers and the Arena for the suffering become a safe place where we can learn to take vulnerability and encouragement into the Big Wide World. You don't have to be a clown to understand this, but if you are it helps!

A Party in Honolulu

The environment of Play can help us to learn valuable lessons and life skills we often forget when we stop being children. The gift of encouragement can draw out even the most hardened and emotionally scarred. Tony Campolo's *The Kingdom of God is a Party* strikes well the note of play and celebration so essential to true release from the ties of legalism and religiosity. He shares a wonderful story that illustrates how the right kind of encouragement can enable even miracles. It's a long section but well worth repeating. Professor Campolo relates how one night staying in a Honolulu hotel he was unable to sleep and so he found himself taking a very early breakfast in a sleazy downtown diner. The story continues:

As I sat there munching on my donut and sipping my coffee at 3.30 in the morning the door of the diner suddenly swung open and, to my discomfort, in marched eight or nine provocative and boisterous prostitutes.

It was a small place and they sat on either side of me. Their talk was loud and crude. I felt completely out of place and was just about to make my getaway when I overheard the woman sitting beside me say, 'Tomorrow's my birthday. I'm going to be thirty-nine.'

Her 'friend' responded in a nasty tone, 'So what do you want from me? A birthday party? What do you want? Ya want me to get you a cake and sing "Happy Birthday"?'

'Come on!' said the woman sitting next to me. 'Why do you have to be so mean? I was just telling you, that's all. Why do you have to put me down? I was just telling you it was my birthday. I don't want anything from you. I mean, why should you give me a birthday party? I've never had a birthday party in my whole life. Why should I have one now?'

When I heard that I made a decision. I sat and waited until the women had left. Then I called over the fat guy behind the counter and I asked him, 'Do they come in here every night?'

'Yeah!' he answered.

'The one right next to me, does she come in here every night?'

'Yeah!' he said. 'That's Agnes. Yeah, she comes in here every night. Why d'ya wanta know?'

'Because I heard her say that tomorrow is her birthday,' I told him. 'What do you say you and I do something about that? What do you think about us throwing a birthday party for her – right here – tomorrow night?'

A cute smile slowly crossed his chubby cheeks and he answered with measured delight, 'That's great! I like it! That's a great idea!' Calling to his wife, who did the cooking in the back room, he shouted, 'Hey! Come out here!

This guy's got a great idea. Tomorrow's Agnes's birthday. This guy wants us to go in with him and throw a birthday party for her – right here – tomorrow night!'

His wife came out of the back room all bright and smiley. She said, 'That's wonderful! You know, Agnes is one of those people who is really nice and kind, and nobody ever does anything nice and kind for her.'

'Look,' I told them. 'If it's O.K. with you, I'll get back here tomorrow morning about 2.30 and decorate the place. I'll even get a birthday cake!'

'No way,' said Harry (that was his name). 'The birthday cake's my thing. I'll make the cake.'

At 2.30 the next morning, I was back at the diner. I had picked up some crepe-paper decorations at the store and had made a sign out of big pieces of cardboard that read, 'Happy Birthday, Agnes!' I decorated the diner from one end to the other. I had that diner looking good.

The woman who did the cooking must have gotten the word out on the street, because by 3.15 every prostitute in Honolulu was in the place. It was wall-to-wall prostitutes . . . and me!

At 3.30 on the dot, the door of the diner swung open and in came Agnes and her friend. I had everyone ready (after all, I was kind of the M.C. of the affair) and when they came in we all screamed 'Happy Birthday!'

Never have I seen a person so flabbergasted . . . so stunned . . . so shaken. Her mouth fell open. Her legs seemed to buckle a bit. Her friend grabbed her arm to steady her. As she was led to one of the stools along the counter we all sang 'Happy Birthday' to her. As we came to the end of our singing with 'happy birthday dear Agnes, happy birthday to you,' her eyes moistened. Then, when the birthday cake with all the candles on it was carried out, she lost it and just openly cried.

Harry gruffly mumbled, 'Blow out the candles, Agnes! Come on! Blow out the candles! If you don't blow out the candles, I'm gonna hafta blow out the candles.' And, after an endless few seconds, he did. Then he handed her a knife and told her, 'Cut the cake, Agnes. Yo, Agnes, we all want some cake.'

Agnes looked down at the cake. Then without taking her eyes off it, she slowly and softly said, 'Look, Harry, is it all right with you if I . . . I mean is it O.K. if I kind of . . . what I want to ask you is . . . is it O.K. if I keep the cake a little while? I mean is it all right if we don't eat it right away?'

Harry shrugged and answered, 'Sure! It's O.K. If you want to keep the cake, keep the cake. Take it home if you want to.'

'Can I?' she asked. Then, looking at me she said, 'I live just down the street a couple of doors. I want to take the cake home, O.K.? I'll be right back. Honest!'

She got off the stool, picked up the cake, and, carrying it like it was the Holy Grail, walked slowly toward the door. As we all sat there motionless, she left.

When the door closed there was a stunned silence in the place. Not knowing what else to do, I broke the silence by saying, 'What do you say we pray?'

Looking back on it now it seems more than strange for a sociologist to be leading a prayer meeting with a bunch of prostitutes in a diner in Honolulu at 3.30 in the morning. But then it just felt like the right thing to do. I prayed for Agnes. I prayed for her salvation. I prayed that her life would be changed and that God would be good to her.

When I finished, Harry leaned over the counter and with a trace of hostility in his voice, he said, 'Hey! You never told me you were a preacher. What kind of church do you belong to?'

In one of those moments when just the right words came, I answered, 'I belong to a church that throws birthday parties for whores at 3.30 in the morning.'

Harry waited for a moment and then almost sneered as he answered, 'No, you don't. There's no church like that. If there was I'd join it! I'd join a church like that!'

Wouldn't we all? Wouldn't we all love to join a church that throws parties for whores at 3.30 in the morning?[2]

Now I'm not saying you have to find a bunch of prostitutes to party with (not unless you want to, that is) but it is a good indicator of the way a bit of creative encouragement, coupled with some divine timing, can work wonders. Think of the kind of positive message Harry would be spreading around his customers and who knows what further miracles followed Professor Campolo's early morning prayer meeting.

Maybe not in Honolulu diners, but in little acts of encouragement, offered in ordinary places, in ordinary ways, we ourselves can start up that upwardly spiralling circle of encouragement.

It's worth a try now, isn't it?

9

THIRD TWIST:
ONCE UPON A TIME

'It was a dark and stormy night. The robber band sat round the smouldering fire, its embers glowing like fireflies in the night. "Tell us a story, chief!" one grizzled robber cried. "Tell us a tale to chill our blood!" So the robber chief began:

' "It was a dark and stormy night. The robber band sat round the smouldering fire . . ." '

And so the story goes on.

When I was young my parents told me, 'Don't tell stories!' If they thought I was making something up or being economical with the truth I would be considered a storyteller and this was not good. 'Telling stories' was a euphemism for telling lies.

Nowadays I tell stories all the time. Being a storyteller is one of my clown gifts. I tell stories in school assemblies and classrooms, in shops and stores, in pubs and clubs and restaurants. I tell stories on the street, I tell stories at home. I even tell stories in church. When I reflect on my career as a storyteller, I think how sad it was that so many of my generation were told: 'Don't tell stories.'

I think the problem may be that stories are

always considered to be fiction and therefore not true. If this is the case then 'David and Goliath' and 'The Conversion of Paul' are not Bible stories; they should perhaps be referred to as 'Scripture narrative'. (Try explaining that to your Sunday school class!) Maybe it would still be OK to call the parables stories because Jesus made them up. But does this make them any less 'true'?

I think, after all, it might be better to stick with the word 'story'.

Yarns, Fables, Tales and Jokes

Stories can be entirely made up out of the storyteller's head or they can be true accounts of actual events. They may be myths, based on fact, or fables with a moral message or purpose to convey. They may be humorous anecdotes, which may or may not be true, and they may be in the shape of jokes. Most of us are intelligent enough to realise that not that many Englishmen, Irishmen and Scotsmen drink together in pubs so frequently! And then there are the famous 'fairy stories', a kind of oral tradition in the West, that we read and see portrayed each year in pantomime. Andersen and Grimm have given us plenty of examples of stories from Europe, and the rest of the world will have their own traditions. Books and films and plays and poems will all contain stories.

Where would we be without Dickens and Shakespeare, Chekov and Austen, Tolkien and Dahl and Blyton? What kind of squalid world would it be without Chaucer and Wordsworth and Tennyson, without Pinter and Christie or Galton and Simpson and Croft and Lloyd? How small our lives would be without stories.

When we go to the pictures or see a play or when we read our children *Snow White* we don't say, 'But of course this isn't true. It's all a lie!' We don't need to. A couple of years ago they brought out a book called: *The Three Little Pigs: the True Story*. It was told from the Big Bad Wolf's perspective and it was very funny. And just as fictional as the original!

We need stories. They form a vital part of our play and they touch all our lives. Many of us love to watch a good quality stand-up comedian telling jokes, or sit in front of our favourite sit-com, for a real good belly laugh. Sometimes, if we're so inclined, we try to tell jokes ourselves when we're with a group of friends or workmates. At St Margaret's our early morning church prayer meeting often ends with a joke. I hope God enjoys them too!

Bedtime stories are great events. Some of us will remember our parents, aunts or uncles reading to us. If we are fortunate we may get the chance to read to our children, grandchildren, nephews and nieces. I remember my teacher reading *The Hobbit* to us in Junior School and it has left me with a love of Tolkien's work to this day. We all reach a time when we think we're too old to have stories read to us but if we're honest, how many of us can resist hearing a good story well told? Obviously not the robber band at the beginning of this chapter.

The novel is still a very popular form of 'playing' and it is good to see the resurgence of the storyteller in a number of areas, particularly schools. I love to tell stories or read aloud from books, attempting to bring life to the characters with different voices and accents and sometimes using action or 'audience participation'. This can be particularly fun in school assemblies, and the communication of Christian truth through stories is a means that holds the interest. It can be wonderful to work with a classroom full of youngsters, developing a story together. We make up the characters and together forge them into a story. A whole variety of means can be used and afterwards the story can be written out, illustrated and displayed!

Books and Films

We have a wealth of wonderful and well-written stories from which to learn. Who could forget the moving story of *The Steadfast Tin Soldier* or *The Little Match Girl*? Margery Williams' book, *The Velveteen Rabbit*, teaches us so much about what it is to be truly loved and *Love You Forever* by Robert Munsch never fails to bring a tear to the eye of the reader with its tale of a parent's love. Television, film and video bring us countless more stories to move and delight us: *Grandpa, The Angel and the Soldier Boy, The Princess Bride.* There are literally thousands of wonderful stories to be read and listened to and thousands more to be made up and narrated.

When I was younger I loved to read and to be read to. I still do. Then it was Edgar Rice Burroughs' *Tarzan*, and *John Carter of Mars,* W.E. Johns' *Biggles* stories, *Sherlock Holmes* and *The Hobbit*. Now it's mainly fantasy and children's stories: Gemmel, Eddings, Tolkien, Brian Jacques, Roald Dahl, Terry Pratchett and, of course, the immortal *Winnie-the-Pooh!*

Many Christian writers have discovered the value of storytelling and the last three decades have seen some very fine examples of the genre. C.S. Lewis, besides being an excellent theologian, was a consummate storyteller and his series, *The Chronicles of Narnia*, will rank high in children's literature. He also wrote adult fantasy. There are many others, from the stirring prose of Calvin Miller to Max Lucado's excellent tales. Walter Wangerin's *The Book of the Dun Cow* and *The Book of Sorrows*, deal strangely and graphically with the themes of sin and evil, repentance and redemption and one of his finest short stories, *The Ragman*, gives a powerful picture of Jesus and the work of the cross.

Jesus the Storyteller

Jesus himself was one of the finest storytellers, of course. What else would you expect from the Word of God! His parables gripped his audience and left them pondering the profundity of their meaning. Many of them were full of humour too. Imagine a man leaving ninety-nine sheep in 'the open field' while he goes to look for one! That would be like a miser leaving ninety-nine fivers on a windy hilltop while he searches for the one he lost on the way up! Think of Jesus standing up at the end of a feast, when everyone had been drinking heavily, and asking loudly, 'Is anyone thirsty?'

Jesus knew the value of the story for communicating truth. He knew that humour lowers barriers and can pierce the heart. He reached out to the poor and the outcast and wove together tales that spoke of matters they understood. Vineyards and sheepfolds, sowing and fishing and raising families. And at the centre of each story was a message that communicated the heart of God.

When we play we will often tell and listen to stories. Sometimes those stories will speak to us of things we would not otherwise receive. Jesus knows that, as we play together, the lessons we learn through stories will reveal truths as profound as any we may glean from work.

Stories and Sermons

Most weeks now I get to tell stories in some shape or form. Sometimes they are jokes or anecdotes and sometimes they are the stories I tell to children during school assemblies. The storytelling I enjoy most however is that which takes place during the preaching which is a regular part of my work. My aim when I do this is not to impart information to my listeners but, hopefully, to enable them to experience God. This is what stories do for us. They draw us into another world where we can experience drama and transcendence, terror and delight, laughter and tears. I don't get upset if people laugh at my sermons; I get upset if they don't. An emotional response, even a negative one, shows that they have been listening. I don't want to be like the preacher who was told by one of his congregation after the service: 'Pastor, did you know there are 234 panes of glass in this church?'

In the Winter issue of *Leadership* (Volume XV, 1994) Pastor Martin Thielen writes of the great value of storytelling in engaging the attention of listeners. Drawing on his experience of the National Storytelling Festival at Jonesborough, Tennessee, he identifies six specific traits that make storytelling so effective. They are Enthusiasm, Animation, Audience Participation, Spontaneity, No Notes and Humour.

Stories are part of our heritage and part of our life. They will always be a part of our play. Whether sacred or secular, biblical or anecdotal, serious or sad, funny or fantastical – stories will always have the power to change us. The last chapter of the last book of C.S. Lewis' *Chronicles of Narnia* ends thus:

> And for us this is the end of all the stories, and we can most truly say that they all lived happily ever after. But for them it was only the beginning of the real story. All their life in this world and all their adventures in Narnia had only been the cover and the title page: now at last they were beginning Chapter One of the Great Story which no one on earth has read: which goes on for ever: in which each chapter is better that the one before.[1]

10

FOURTH TWIST:
THE GAMES WE PLAY

What is it about play that is so conducive to a more relaxed lifestyle? For one thing I suppose it's natural: something built into us from the beginning. It meets a deep emotional need that neither a well paid job nor even regular church attendance can fulfil. We all need it and, if we're honest, we all like it. I heard of a top executive who, unwilling for his colleagues to know he wasn't working, called his yacht *Conference* so that, if anyone phoned his office, his secretary could truthfully say: 'I'm afraid he's not available today, he's in *Conference*'!

One interesting bridge between work and play is in the area of games. At the level of blind-man's buff and cops and robbers they are very close to the sphere of play. At the level of Premier League soccer and Formula One motor racing they are well into the arena of work. In his fascinating best-seller *Games People Play*, Dr Eric Berne gives the following definition of games:

A game is an ongoing series of complementary ulterior transactions progressing to a well-defined, predictable outcome. Descri-ptively it is a recurring set of transactions, often repetitious, superficially plausible, with a concealed motivation; or, more colloquially, a series of moves with a snare, or 'gimmick'. Games are clearly differentiated from procedures, rituals and pastimes by two chief characteristics: (1) their ulterior quality and (2) the payoff.[1]

And there I was thinking hide-and-seek was simple!

Games bridge the gap between Work and Play, as we shall see, because they usually, though not always, are a means to an end. Take the games we watch, for example.

Games, Quizzes and Game Shows

We love to participate in games and we love to watch others do so. Whether they are physical games like football and squash, pastimes like coin collecting or needlepoint or board games like Scrabble or Risk. Monopoly is still the most popular board game and the game of Ludo was taken from the Greek 'to play'. Trivial Pursuit exploits the love many of us have for quizzes. Up and down the country many pubs and clubs have quiz teams and radio and television quizzes like *Brain of Britain, Mastermind* and *A Question of Sport* attract large audiences. Every weekday afternoon some four million plus viewers tune in to Channel 4's first and ever popular quiz: *Countdown.*

In the last twenty years the TV game show has become a very popular form of play, originating in the States. Huge prizes are often offered and many will switch on simply for the vicarious pleasure of sharing in somebody else's dream. The shows become more and more spectacular, seeking ever more creative ways of entertaining the public's desire to play games. I know; I've been on a couple myself. We've come a long way from the days when Michael Miles invited you to 'Take Your Pick'.

'Would you like the treasure chest containing *fifty* pounds?' 'Yes!' Ding!

There's no doubt that we like to play – when we have the time, of course! Sometimes our play can be tainted by the desire to make money. The game shows increasingly pander to this and an ill-advised trip to Las Vegas in 1998 showed me how far some people will go in 'playing the wheel' or the slot machine! The last couple of years have seen the introduction in Britain of the National Lottery, ostensibly set up to help the less well off and creating dozens of temporary millionaires and millions of disappointed punters. Gambling, whether with one armed bandits or scratch cards, is not real play because it has an ulterior motive and can never be an end in itself. This kind of 'play' is more like work, with its emphasis on achievement, and so it can never truly provide fulfilment. Most hardened gamblers (the truthful ones, at least) will tell you that gambling is a gaping vacuum, an unsatisfied black hole that consumes the consumer and gives nothing in return.

Super Mario and Sonic the Hedgehog
Another kind of game that has rapidly increased in popularity with the ICT revolution is the video game. I must confess I enjoy video games, especially the ones where you get to knock seven bells out of someone else's dinosaur/robot/ninja! Many things can be learned from video games not least of

which is that the best form of conflict resolution is not knocking seven bells out of your opponent! However, I have three major hang ups with Nintendo, Sega and the rest.

First: their prices. Games should be fun; they should also be easily accessible to all. The big video game manufacturers are exploiting children and parents by charging prices that are unreasonable and unfair for their CDs, cassettes and consoles. Peer pressure often pushes children and parents into unnecessary debt. Second is the growing obsession with horror, violence and sex. Some of the more graphic video games can only qualify as soft porn in terms of blood and naked flesh. Censorship seems inadequate since many of these games are showing in public arcades and dealers can sometimes be none too careful in sales to minors. Lastly, video games are often solitary play items and individuals can spend hours, glued to a screen without any other human contact. There is certainly some value in challenging other people, or even the machine itself but an unremitting diet of 'solitary play' video games will be worse than never having played at all.

Competition and Co-operation

What really matters in life, as I've already said, is not what we do, but who we are. Play is not primarily about acquisition or achievement. This heart-warming story from the States illustrates that fact perfectly:

A few years ago at the Seattle Special Olympics, nine contestants all physically or mentally disabled, assembled at the starting line for the 100 yard dash. At the gun, they all started out, not exactly in a dash, but with a relish to run the race to the finish and win. All, that is, except one boy who stumbled on the asphalt, tumbled over a couple of times, and began to cry. The other eight heard the boy cry. They slowed down and looked back. They all turned around in unison and went back – every one of them. One girl with Down's Syndrome bent down and kissed him and said, 'This will make it better.' All nine competitors linked arms and walked across the finish line together. Everyone in the stadium stood and the cheering went on for several minutes. People who were there are still telling the story. Why? Because deep down we all know this one truth: What matters in this life is more than winning for ourselves. What truly matters in this life is helping others to win, even if it means slowing down and changing our course.

Games will be one of the most important constituents of Play. They make up a large part of my Clowning Workshops, and they are one of the most constant features of our play as children. We may also see that they play a not insignificant part in our lives as adults.

As children we unconsciously learn many of our life skills through the playing of games. We learn to co-operate in teams, to give and take from one another. We learn to run and jump and skip and hop. We learn the strengths and weaknesses of our bodies. We learn the value of relationships. We learn to laugh.

We also learn to compete with one another and to sulk when we can't get our own way or when others beat us. We learn to hurt and be hurt. In our games we mimic and imitate what we think we might do in reality as adults. We copy the heroes of TV and video and we imagine ourselves to be famous pop idols or sports stars.

We learn much through games, a great deal of it being put into practice in later life. Without the time for play, particularly in the area of games we lose many opportunities for learning. A recent study of children at play in school showed that where there was less play because of the pressures of curriculum, there was consequently less chance for the development of social and inter-personal skills such as conflict resolution. Most schools have known for some time the great value of play, and not just as a means for teachers to have a few minutes peace and children to let off a bit of steam. Games and play are valuable in themselves. Play areas and activity centres are increasing in schools and nurseries and even in shopping centres. A number of councils are taking the time and money to ensure their parks and recreation grounds are maintained and with good, clean, creative, safe play areas.

When the opportunity to play games is curtailed or removed we may find ourselves lacking in the kind of inter-personal skills we normally take for granted. One result is an inability to engage in 'small-talk', another is an unwillingness to cope with conflict or deferment of confrontation. In themselves they may seem small items but they can easily lead to relationships that are solely task-driven. When small-talk is eliminated, there is no need to interact with another person for the sake of friendship but only in as far as that will accomplish a given task or desire. When true conflict-resolution is shunned, there is no room for repentance or forgiveness. In the long run, un-neighbourliness, family feuding, employment strikes and sit-ins, separation and divorce and even internecine war can follow, in ascending (or descending!) order. Inability to play or lack of opportunity for games cannot be solely blamed for the above but they may have a bigger role than we think.

Games and Relationships

Nowhere is the playing of games seen more clearly as in that most personal of interpersonal relationships: that between a man and a woman. John Gray's best seller, *Men are from Mars, Women are from Venus* has been very influential in this area. The premise of the book is that men and women are from two different planets with very different behaviour patterns. When they discovered each other they immediately moved to earth where they quickly forgot their origins. This cleverly explains the inherent differences in the ways men and women relate and an understanding of this can lead to improved communication and better relationships. John Gray says, 'Love is magical, and it can last, if we remember our differences.'[2]

Courtship is unquestionably a very popular game and the games continue into marriage. Understanding this fact is a major step forward; realising the rules of the games, and how to play most effectively, can lead to greatly enhanced relationships. The phrases: 'playing the field' and 'playing hard to get' spring to mind in the area of courtship, and many of us will know how closely we must adhere to the rules in this kind of game! As opposed to football or even Monopoly, those most serious of games, in this game the stakes are so high they could change your life forever.

John Gray shows us that understanding the differences between men and women can make an enormous amount of difference in the game of life. Women, for example, tend to be empathisers. They like to meet together to discuss their feelings. Men, on the other hand, are problem solvers. They like to single-handedly provide the solution. Because the man always counters the woman's concerns with his 'answers' she complains he isn't listening. When the woman tries to help the man accomplish his task better, he complains she is trying to change him. She wants to nurture; he feels controlled. He wants to help; she feels ignored. The men, who originate from Mars, are goal orientated. The women, who originate from Venus, are relationship orientated. Men and women both fluctuate in their relationship and go through 'seasons'. This, too, needs to be rightly understood. John Gray writes:

> Life is filled with rhythms – day and night, hot and cold, summer and winter, spring and fall, cloudy and clear. Likewise in a relationship, men and women have their own rhythms and cycles. Men pull back and then get close, while women rise and fall in their ability to love themselves and others.[3]

Men are from Mars, Women are from Venus tells the story of a knight in shining armour rescuing a damsel in distress from a dragon. When the rescue is repeated a second and a third time the damsel offers repeated advice as to how the knight might accomplish his task better. As a result the knight feels undermined and weakened. After a while he goes off to rescue another damsel in distress and doesn't return. Had the woman understood a little more of the man, and had the man understood a little more of the woman, it need never have happened.

The different approaches to life made by men and women can be disguised somewhat in the field of work, but in the area of play they are all too apparent. Clearly, not enough work has been done in the preparation of men and women for the permanent and binding relationship of marriage. In this most critical of 'games' relationships are seen as being increasingly disposable, resulting in horrendous loss of trust and a return to cynicism and coldness. The problem is that the rules of the game have been set aside and so the game can no longer be played. What should be the most enjoyable activity in the field of play and the highest degree of relationship becomes instead a battlefield where few prisoners are taken and amnesties are seldom declared.

There are a number of excellent resources available in this area if we but took the trouble to seek them. Rob Parsons' book, *The Sixty Minute Marriage*, is one; John Gray's work is another. The former's book is crammed with loads of funny, tearful, wisdom and you can read it in an hour. If your mating game is going off the rails (and even if it just needs a bit of renewal) get Rob's book and read it. And get your partner to read it too! Here's just a flavour. The 'One Second Page': 'It may not always be right to stay together "for the sake of the children". But it's still a good reason.'[4]

John Gray's book takes longer to read but is

equally good. We owe it to one another to purify our games and make the most of our relationships. I often wonder as the 'happy couple' stand in front of me at the sanctuary step to pledge 'I will', whether this relationship will last. Will Dave and Sharon become just another statistic on a list of failures and will theirs be the children whose parents have different addresses? I hope not. We need to do all we can to safeguard the family and the home or the consequences may be with us for considerably more than a single lifetime.

It is undoubtedly true that playing games improves our 'people skills'. The most valuable time for learning is while we are children but there is still much we can learn as adults. Admittedly, when we grow up we tend to call our games 'sport', but we can treat them just as seriously as a six-year-old regards 'chasing on the white line' or 'off ground tag'. Just observe the reactions of a group of adults watching football, snooker or tennis on TV and tell me that sport is not a deadly serious business. It brings to mind the late Bill Shankly's famous comment that football is not a matter of life and death; it's far more important than that!

The games we play as adults go far beyond the football field and golf course, however. Playing games with each other leads us into an area that is more child*ish* than child*like*. We find it in offices and factories; we find it in the home. We also find plenty of it in churches. Consciously and unconsciously, we play our little games with one another where the only goal is to advance ourselves and further our own ambitions.

The games we play are not to be played alone or

to give us personal advantage over others. They are not to manipulate or coerce nor are they ultimately to decide supremacy. Games are not really part of the 'leisure industry'; they are part of play and quite distinct from work. The games we play teach us to enjoy one another and ourselves: to learn to live and interact joyfully with each other. They are participated in with fun and laughter. They are an expression of the creative Creator who placed within us the capacity to play, to join with him in his creativity. To indulge ourselves in re-creation.

11

FIFTH TWIST:
LAUGHTER – THE BEST MEDICINE

Somebody once told me it takes twice as many muscles in your face to frown as it does to smile. Actually the ratio is 17 to 43 in favour of the smile. A clown told me if you turn your mouth up at the edges it's a whole lot easier to carry around!

Smiles and laughter (coupled with love) are part of what makes life worth living. I guess that's what you'd expect to hear from a clown if not from a vicar. A clown's life is dedicated to helping people laugh whereas a vicar's life is dedicated to helping people live. I think they both have the job of calling people to love. Laughter is the atmosphere, the realm, in which we play. It can be tremendously liberating.

There is so much that can sadden and depress us in this 'valley of tears' we call our life. To embrace the gift of laughter and even to laugh at ourselves is like water poured on thirsty ground. It brings refreshment and renewal. One of the saddest stories in the Bible, the tale of Job, contains more mention of laughter than any other book. The desolate Job is reminded: 'He will yet fill your mouth with laughter and your lips with shouts of joy' (Job 8:21).

Laughing in Church

Even in the midst of overwhelming sorrow, laughter can bring healing and peace. Too often we consider it a trivial thing, something for the inane and the insane. A chuckle or belly laugh is thought to be beneath many people and giggling is something only children should indulge in. In many areas laughter in church is considered wholly inappropriate. (It is of course 'holy' appropriate!) It always strikes me as strange that judges and doctors and bishops and the like are always expected to be solemn and serious as though smiles and laughter were indications of shallowness. I would have thought that a bright and smiling face, coupled with a sunny disposition, is far more likely to put people at ease, be they in a courtroom, surgery or cathedral.

I know a vicar in Liverpool who was castigated by his congregation for daring to smile and wish them 'Good morning' at the beginning of the service. How daft can you get! I know of other churches where a joke in the sermon would be considered extremely bad form. Such 'po-faced' attitudes remind me of an old *Punch* cartoon I saw years ago. Imagine the scene: a crusty old Bishop, resplendent in frock coat and gaiters, is accosted outside the cathedral one bright May morning by his eager-to-please Archdeacon. Gazing up at the sky and beaming brightly the latter remarks, 'Spring in the air, Bishop.' 'Hrrummp!' grumbles his lordship testily. 'Spring in the air yourself, Archdeacon!'

I do tend to laugh and smile a lot, I'll grant you, and not just because I'm a clown. I find that humour is the key to unlock many a cold heart. Can I be the only one to address supermarket checkout operators and waiters in restaurants by the name so clearly printed on their lapel badge? Surely it can only be there so that customers like me can pass the time of day with them, find out how they are and make the tedious business of checking bar codes and totalling menus a little easier. And is there really anything wrong with saying 'Hello' to the bus driver when you get on the vehicle, or thanking the train guard for a pleasant trip? A bright smile and perhaps a humorous word, pitched at the right level, can make all the difference in our frantic noisy existence. We've all met the superficially cheery waitress who greets her fifteenth family of the day with: 'Hello. My name's Tracy and I'll be your waitress for the evening.' Why not smile brightly and say: 'Good evening Tracy! My name's John and this is my wife Kim. We'll be your customers for the evening.' (Substitute your own names of course!) If nothing else it breaks the ice; cuts through some of poor Tracy's monotony and could make for some quite pleasant conversation. Hopefully, you'll have made a new friend.

The Small Pleasures of Life

Chantal (not her real name), a French girl working in London from 7 am to 7 pm, is not allowed lunch breaks. 'It's much harder than Paris,' she says. 'People are eliminating the small pleasures of life.'

The 'small pleasures of life' include the joy of seeing a face light up in response to your smile or quip. Be honest now – is it not true that a cheery face and bright personality behind the counter of your local garage lifts your outlook on the day? In his short story *Edification/Demolition*, Walter

Wangerin tells of two service-station attendants he
encountered with two very different attitudes: one
positive and one negative. One made him smile;
the other made him sad. We may think the everyday encounters we have are of little consequence.
Walter Wangerin writes:

> But I say to you: 'Every time you meet another
> human being you have the opportunity. It's a
> chance at holiness. For you will do one of two
> things, then. Either you will build him up, or
> you will tear him down.'[1]

It's not so difficult to make people smile. Smiling at
them helps. Saying: 'Hello, how are you?' and
'Thank you!' are small courtesies but make a world
of difference in 'the small pleasures of life'. You
don't have to be a clown to understand this, but if
you are it helps!

I'm sure I can't be the only one who gets the
infuriatingly clueless telephonist when I call up a
large company. Admittedly, you have to get
through all the automated stuff first. 'If you wish to
place an order please press button 1, if you've
changed your address please press button 2, if you
want to swear at the manager please press button
8, thank you for your patience . . .' – that kind of
thing. Finally you get through to a real person. But
are they? You try very hard to convey your cheery
smile down the phone. You even try to build some
kind of relationship but you soon realise you're
getting nowhere. You would have got more sense
out of the automated message. The thing is – don't
give up! Resist the urge to press button 8. Keep
smiling that bright winsome smile and be polite!

Who knows – even clueless telephonists may discover a sense of humour!

Healing Humour

In recent years the medical profession has discovered the therapeutic value of laughter. Some hospitals even employ clowns to entertain the patients and make them laugh. (What a great job – I wonder how much they pay?) Research shows that people who laugh heal quicker! A smile and a bright and positive attitude can work wonders in restoring people's health. The book of Proverbs says: 'All the days of the oppressed are wretched, but the cheerful heart has a continual feast' (Proverbs 15:15) and: 'A cheerful heart is good medicine, but a crushed spirit dries up the bones' (Proverbs 17:22).

It seems to me that hospitals should be places not for the sick but for the recovering; somewhere they treat the person and not just the condition. This is the kind of distinction that says an individual has value regardless of what they can do for others or what value they have to society as a whole. It makes patients into people and customers can even become friends. In this kind of environment laughter is a natural expression of positive relationship.

The first ever NHS Laughter Clinic was opened in 1991 for the West Birmingham Health Authority by counsellor Robert Holden and in Oxford he now runs The Happiness Project, which seeks to improve the quality of life by exploring what it means to be really happy. As part of the therapy Robert teaches various subtle strategies, the first of which is to begin taking the world and ourselves less seriously. The first step he teaches his groups is simply to laugh out loud! Research proves laughter helps you get well. It provides a physical workout; exercising heart and lungs, improving blood flow and relaxing tension. It releases catecholemines, which are thought to reduce inflammation, and raises the level of immunoglobin A, an antibody which marks bacteria for destruction by white blood cells. In addition, a real good belly laugh floods the system with enkephalins, the body's own pain-suppressing agents.

A Generation of Grumps

Old people, they tell me, can be notoriously grumpy. Jack Lemon and Walter Matthau did an excellent job of it in *Grumpy Old Men* and *Grumpier Old Men.* I've not generally found it to be the case. Most of the old people I know are fairly cheerful, much like most of the children I know, in fact. Youngsters and oldsters are, in the main, fairly similar in their approach to life. The former live in the eternal now where history is five minutes ago and the latter live in the past, since the present is uncomfortable and the future not worth thinking about. Both see their perspective through rose-tinted glasses: either the glorious and fascinating world of the present or the fabled 'good old days'.

No, it's my generation that are the grumpy ones, passionless and unenthusiastic and often with little or no sense of humour. It seems to be sucked out somewhere in early teens when dreams die and people contract reality sickness. It's those of us in our so-called 'middle years' (somewhere between puberty and senility) that have the most to answer for. We're the ones with all the stress and busyness and angst. We're the complaining generation, the disgruntled and dissatisfied: largely without vision and without leadership. And, sadly, without much laughter either. It doesn't have to be like that.

Sarai and Abram were an elderly Jewish couple, who had a dream of having a family, just like many today. Trouble is, they'd been trying for decades and now they were both well past it. Sarai even suggested hubby should try it on with the maid and see if that got them anywhere. (I don't know, these old timers!) Anyway, one day God told the old chap they would have a son! Furthermore, their names would be changed from Abram to Abraham, which means, 'father of many', and Sarai would become Sarah, which means 'princess'. Imagine – calling a ninety-year-old 'princess'! And as for having a son! The old lady laughed to even think of it. But a year later their son was born and they named him 'laughter'. I can't help grinning as I think of those two old dears with their arms around each other, cradling their infant son and laughing fit to bust!

Laughing Places

In the wonderful Brer Rabbit stories, Uncle Remus tells the children about the rascally rodent's 'laughing place'. Everybody has one he tells them. 'Trouble is, most folks won't take the time to go look for it. And what it is for one it mightn't be for another!' We all have different things, people, or situations that make us laugh. The important thing is that we laugh. That we take the time to go find that laughing place and when we get there – set a spell!

Laughter is not always appropriate, of course. There are times when we need to keep a straight face, even when the rest of the world is crooked. At times, laughter can be positively dangerous. In Umberto Eco's now famous story, *The Name of the Rose,* the Venerable Yorge swiftly despatches anyone who wants to read a book on laughter, supposedly written by Aristotle. Yorge does this because he considers that laughter frees us from fear of God's law and, if we do not reverence and submit to God's law then the world will descend into chaos. But Law must be balanced by Grace and formality by spontaneity. The letter may kill, but the Spirit gives life. Clowns weep through their laughter and laugh through their tears.

Jean-Jacques Suurmond writes:

> In laughter human beings transcend their bond with the world and relativize this without escaping it. However, those who take themselves too seriously, who cannot play or laugh continue to coincide with the world and cannot transcend it. Therefore those who can laugh at themselves are the freest and most human.[2]

Learning to Laugh

It is the Christian Church, most of all that needs to teach the world to laugh. Let's face it: most churches are funny places and, to the outsider, the services we run and the things we do are hilarious. Imagine, where else do you find grown men and women running around in fancy dress and saying such amusing things? (OK – so the House of Lords can be quite funny too!) The scope for humour in the church is immense. 'Next week's preacher will be found pinned to the notice board.' 'Will ladies with eggs for Harvest Festival please lay them in the font.' 'Now, choir: Nice and loud. Tenors: when we get to "the gates of hell", you come in.' And then there was the little girl who felt ill during the intercessions so her mother sent her out of the service. She soon returned feeling much better. Apparently, she'd discovered a bowl in the porch marked 'For the Sick'! I could go on . . . but perhaps I'd better not.

There have been a number of hilarious books published in the realm of so-called 'religious humour'. Murray Watts' *Rolling in the Aisles* and *Bats in the Belfry,* Bob Phillips' *Jest Another Good Clean Joke Book,* Nick Mercer and Stephen Gaukroger's *Frogs in Cream* (I and II) and Martin Wroe, Nick McIvor and Simon Parke's *101 things to do with a Dull Church* are good examples of the 'quick-fire' jokes. Adrian Plass has delighted us with a whole range of humorous stories, particularly his *Sacred Diary* series and Bob Jackson's *Till the Fat Lady Sings* is both moving and hilarious. And can we ever forget the outrageous statement made by the clergyman who said 'There's nothing better than curling up in bed with a good Trollope'? Yes, I think we'd better! Forget it, I mean!

It shouldn't surprise us that humour is at home in church. After all, in dramatic terms the Christian faith is a comedy not a tragedy. Jesus' life didn't end on a cross but rising from a tomb and living forever. If you've ever read the Bible through to the last page you'll find it has a happy ending. Is it any wonder that in the Greek Orthodox tradition they still meet together to tell jokes on the second day of Easter! Just think of the quips: 'Have you heard the one about the empty tomb? There's nothing in it!'

Laughter is, I'm happy to say, infectious. In

other words, you can catch it. You don't have to touch people with it or even have them breathe heavily on you. You just have to be near them and you're immediately at risk. Now it is possible to build up immunity to laughter. Soulless office work or repetitive factory jobs will do it. Spending lots of time with cynical and disillusioned people will certainly help. Spurning belief and values and vision and drive and reckoning the world owes you a living and that other people are there for your benefit. That'll certainly push you a long way down the road to invulnerability. But the good news is that nobody can be completely immune.

Nobody.

12

SIXTH TWIST: PLAYGROUNDS

There's nothing quite like a fairground or theme park to bring out the child in us. They're great places for play and we can learn a lot from them. But it's not all good. They can be noisy and smelly and they will usually have a depreciating effect upon the wallet. At times, they can also be pretty scary!

A Trip to the Magic Mountain

One of the most terrifying places on the planet must surely be Six Flags Magic Mountain, just north of Los Angeles, California. It's a rollercoaster park for grownups and it is usually filled with hordes of strangely-dressed teenagers all pushing past each other to be first in the queue for the newest 'vomit comet'. In a moment of what I can only describe as middle-age madness I allowed my thirteen-year-old son, Ben, to persuade me to take him during our US holiday in the summer of 1998. I say 'madness', because Ben informed me that far from allowing his poor grey-haired old dad to sit serenely by, vicariously spectating, I would be required to participate. If I didn't go with him, my dear son informed me, his school friends would find out and I would be branded a wimp and no one can hold up their head in class whose dad is a wimp!

You see what I mean by madness? My head must have been softened by the Californian sun for me to be taken in by such a story. However, partly out of love for my children, and partly taken in by the blandishments of my wife ('Don't worry, sweetheart, we'll be able to sneak off somewhere') I rose early in the morning to take my family to Six Flags. What a hero! What a fool!

Six Flags Magic Mountain is a large theme park that is most definitely not designed for 'pregnant women and those suffering from neck or back problems'. Neither is it entirely suitable for those of a nervous disposition or those who wish to retain their previous meal. It is certainly not advisable for anyone suffering from any kind of chronic fatigue disorder. 'Like me,' I told Ben, 'like me!' The argument wouldn't wash. I didn't want the youth of Stanford thinking I was a mouse did I? . . . Squeak!

As we walked up towards the entrance gates and saw the huge brightly coloured metal monsters towering above the perimeter fences, catapulting their flailing, screaming victims around at breakneck speeds I could already feel my back and neck muscles tensing and my stomach beginning to lurch. There was the Superman, a horrendous vertical drop from what seemed like thousands of feet, backwards, at over 100 mph! There was the Centrifuge that spun you round so fast you'd feel like your eyes were popping out while your breakfast was saying hello to your tonsils for the second time. And there was the Skydive (for which you had to actually pay extra!) that dropped you in a cradle, either alone or with a couple of other brain-dead individuals, on a huge pendulum that swung you, screaming insanely, over the heads of the astonished onlookers. Worst of all, they advertised the newest torture: The Riddler's Revenge, an iridescent green and yellow behemoth billed as the fastest tallest stand-up rollercoaster in the world. Stand-up!? And to think, we were paying to go in here!

Some judicious use of the toilets, the occasional lingering over my fizzy drink and (yes, I'll admit it!) quite a bit of hiding, managed to delay the awful moment. But it wasn't to be put off forever. The hour of doom arrived all too soon and I found myself standing with Ben in the interminable queue for . . . what was it? Oh no! The Riddler's Revenge!

Now, I'm good at queueing. I've had plenty of practice in Disneyworld. Clowns are good at faces and I was well able to alternate between the cool matter-of-fact 'this is all a bit of a doddle for me' face and the suave sophisticated 'Rollercoasters? Yeah! Been on 'em all' face. And then we actually began to get near the head of the queue, nearer to the moment of departure. The sadistic swines who had designed this apparatus had actually planned it so that the queue passed right underneath the rails of the speeding monster so that, every forty seconds or so, a huge deafening roar filled the ears as another batch of shrieking teenagers hurtled above. As I stared at the twisting, looping, plunging carriages, transfixed like a mouse in the hypnotic gaze of a snake, I expected at any moment to see a piece of metal, a stray camera or hat or some arms and legs come flying off into the crowd below.

'Smile, John; this is fun!'

All too soon I was there. A grinning student, who must surely have known the sweat running copiously down my back wasn't just from the heat of the sun, was thrusting me into the belly of the beast. The harness comes down; I make a last desperate attempt to hold onto my stomach and bowels. In that fleeting instant I know I've made a terrible mistake. 'Blow what the youth of Stanford think, or my congregation or my friends. I am a wimp! I don't care who knows. I can't face six double loops, seven twists, five 100-foot drops at speeds over 65 miles an hour and they won't even let me sit down! Ben can get a stand-in dad, one who does rollercoasters. Let me off! I'm out of here!!'

But it's all too late. With a gut-wrenching jolt we're off! Two minutes of plunging, twisting, turning, speeding, zooming, soaring, rollercoasting later we're back and Ben and I get off.

'Wow! That was absolutely great! When can we do it again, Ben?!'

Yes, we can learn a lot from playing in theme parks. Life can be a bit of a rollercoaster, filled with ups and downs. Often, you have a sense of being out of control, of not being in charge of the direction you're taking. There may be times of quiet desperation as we await an imagined event or moments of sheer terror as we feel about to be plummeted into catastrophe. More often than not, the imagined disaster does not occur and we may, in retrospect, even be exhilarated by the experience.

In *Parenthood* (the Steve Martin film), the dear little old granny of the family is given perhaps the most profound insight to share:

> You know, when I was nineteen, grandpa took me on a rollercoaster. Up . . . down, up . . . down. Oh, what a ride! I always wanted to go again. You know, it was just interesting to me that a ride could make me so frightened, so scared, so sick, so excited and so thrilled all together. Some didn't like it – they went on the merry-go-round. But that just goes around . . . nothing! I like the rollercoaster. You get more out of it.

Swings and Roundabouts

When we played as children much of our play took place at the local playground or park. There would be swings and a seesaw and, if we were lucky, a roundabout as well. We'd spend hours with our friends just enjoying our play. Nowadays, these same areas are called adventure playgrounds and include many more different types of activities and, I'm very pleased to say, a variety of safety features as well. I'm only sorry for that notice that tells me I'm too old to use the equipment! Ah, well – there's always the theme parks.

A great deal of what we learned as youngsters about relationships we picked up in the play area. Sometimes play was wonderful and exciting. Sometimes it was miserable and horrid. Like the time we fell off the swing and grazed a knee or when no one picked us to be on their team in the football match. And sometimes we played great games with our friends and sometimes we argued and fought and sulked and cried. I do wonder if life as an adult is vastly different. Sometimes it's great and sometimes it's horrid. Life has its ups and downs, a bit like the rollercoaster. There is the exhilaration of a closed deal or a family celebration. There is the pain of a broken friendship or an unexpected argument. Life still comes in waves, in work, rest and play. There are ups and downs, good times and bad. Kipling calls triumph and disaster 'two impostors' that we should treat alike. We can try to avoid the ups and downs, stay on the roundabouts, if you like: the slower, quieter attractions. But we may just find that life would be missing something very valuable. The rollercoasters teach us perspective. And perspective shows us how to live.

The seesaws are important too for, in addition to perspective, they teach us balance. The strange phrase 'swings and roundabouts' is actually talking about what the seesaw does. Even stranger, the fun comes when you are either up or down because you know that in a short while you will be moving. There is no fun in a seesaw that is not moving. One that is in perfect balance, neither moving up or down, is not worth bothering with. It was all very well having your big sister or Fatty Roberts from 5C on the other end but, unless you had two of your mates with you on your end, you were going to be stuck up in the air for a while. The fun of the seesaw (or 'teeter totter', as the Americans call it) is the anticipation of suddenly changing direction. The lesson of the seesaw is not that balance is boring, immobile stability but that it is a constantly shifting readjustment.

Do you remember trying to adjust too quickly and overdoing it? The seesaw came down onto the pitted tarmac or turf with a great thud. And didn't that hurt your rear end? Sometimes it made you shout with laughter, and sometimes it made you cry with pain. Changing direction can do that just as effectively, though, perhaps not as dramatically, as the rollercoaster. Balance is a dynamic not a fixed point. We need to be constantly evaluating and making readjustments in order to maintain it. It can be fun and it can be frightening. The seesaw teaches us that.

I still think my favourite piece of equipment in the playground is the swing. There is nothing quite so wonderful as swinging to and fro and letting the world go by. When we were very young we were sat in those special swings with plastic guards round so we couldn't fall off and, since we were unable to make it move unaided, an adult pushed it for us – usually Mum or Dad. I can still remember the great joy that came the first time I learned that, by moving your legs in a certain way, I was able to operate the swing on my own and determine the speed and height I went. I have also been able to relive the pleasure through my children and hope to again through my grandchildren. There is something very special about just swinging backwards and forwards, one second seeing the ground and the next seeing the sky, with all the variety of landscape in between. Perhaps the thrill comes from movement without going anywhere thus being an activity that can be enjoyed for its own sake. The Downs Syndrome children I used to work and play with would often rock to and fro, imitating the movement of the swing. Perhaps they had discovered an action without a goal that could be enjoyed for itself.

Even having learned to swing unassisted there is still something thrilling about having someone push you. There's the confidence in the person you know and the slightly fearful anticipation of the one less well known. Max Lucado writes about this in one of his short stories from *On the Anvil*. He notes that Jesus was unafraid in the storm on the lake because he knew who was 'pushing the swing'. He continues:

> Everywhere I look, private storms occur. Family deaths, strained marriages, broken hearts, lonely evenings. We must remember who is pushing the swing. We must put our trust in him. We can't grow fearful. He won't let us tumble out.
>   Who pushes your swing? In the right hands, you can find peace . . . even in the storm.[1]

When we trust the one who's pushing the swing we can hang on and have fun.

I could talk about slides and tree houses, whirligigs and helter-skelters and a myriad of other equipment we could find in playground, fairground and theme park. Perhaps the greatest lesson we can learn from them is that they enable us to engage in meaningless activity that can be enjoyed for its own sake. Even to use the word 'meaningless' is pejorative for it implies uselessness. Nevertheless, play is not intended to be productive. If it were, it would be work. We do not play primarily because we wish to achieve something. We play because we enjoy it: because it's fun.

Holy Play
Playgrounds are actually holy places. When we

take off our shoes and socks and leap into the sand-pit we are standing in the footsteps of Moses and Joshua. As we run and jump and shout and play, we may be touching the faces of angels.

In his groundbreaking book *Word and Spirit at Play*, Dutch Reformed minister, Jean-Jacques Suurmond contrasts play with charismatic worship. He uses J. Huzinga's definition of play from the latter's book, *Homo Ludens, A Study of the Play Element in Culture*:

> Play is a voluntary activity or occupation executed within certain fixed limits of time and place, according to rules freely accepted but absolutely binding, having its aim in itself, accompanied by a feeling of tension, joy and the consciousness that it is 'different' from 'ordinary life'.[2]

Were we not told that this is a definition of Play, we might even consider this to be a description of some aspects of charismatic worship. Pastor Suurmond pushes the analogy further. He contrasts the services of many Pentecostal assemblies where attendance is *'a voluntary occupation'*, pursued with great joy and not out of guilt, duty or compulsion as in some more established churches where the emphasis is on order. The charismatic celebration, like the game, is played out within a fixed time and place, often in a particular building that has no other particular use. He comments that the day of worship (typically a Sunday) has tended to lose some of its holy set apart character, taking on more of a legalistic and regulated, rather than prophetic nature. Sunday then becomes only a means to an end and no different from a working day. People who do not go to church but instead play sport or engage in other forms of recreation are celebrating the Sabbath in a far more real way than the Christians who have reduced it to another day for achievement.

Just as play has binding rules, so liturgy and worship have their rules, 'freely accepted but absolutely binding'. However, no child at play concentrates so utterly on the rules that the game is no longer enjoyable. In many of our churches, an over-emphasis on order and regulation has killed the spirit of worship. We are no longer able to 'play' in our worship because the Word has not been made flesh. The intellectual has smothered the emotional and the letter has strangled the life. Pastor Suurmond points out that if the formal rites can serve the liturgical game, rather than dominating it, then the elements of charismatic worship such as 'parables, humour, glossolalia and the foolishness of other charismatic expressions' can enable and release us to truly worship God in spirit as well as in truth. It may well be that Pentecostal congregations and the more established churches (particularly Anglicans and Catholics) can learn from each other about properly balancing liturgy and spontaneity in this wonderful game of celebration worship. This may help to release both the more traditional forms of worship from heaviness and formalism and the newer Pentecostal churches from excess and fundamentalism.

In celebration we waste time before God. Like play, worship of God has 'its aim in itself'. Jean-Jacques Suurmond writes:

Only in the useless play of celebration is life taken seriously as a true gift of God. Here God's kingdom already breaks through to some extent, so that the celebration is itself both already eternal life (the Eastern Orthodox view) and the means to salvation and liberation (the Roman-Catholic view). Here, through the Word and the Spirit, God's people are increasingly tuned to the eternal sabbath play so that the celebration in principle has power to change the world. A celebration makes you human again, since the game is fundamentally for our humanity.[3]

Once we grasp the idea that God is 'useless' because he is *not* a means but an end in himself, then we begin to be able to move away from the purpose-orientated habits of the working week. Work, as I have already tried to show, needs to be purposeful and with a clear aim. Play, on the other hand, is purposeless for its aim is in itself. In the same way, those who join in charismatic celebration give themselves to one another and to God as free gifts of grace.

Huzinga's definition is further pressed to explore the feelings of 'tension' and 'joy'. In charismatic celebration people are released to 'play the play of the kingdom of God'. This can allow huge creativity and involve all of the senses: sight (banners and stained-glass windows), sound (music and song), smell (incense and candles), taste (bread and wine), touch (other people!). This list of course is not exhaustive. The celebration may be both intense and joyful. Dance, particularly spontaneous dance, will often be a feature of this kind of worship and Pastor Suurmond suggests this as 'one of the purest and most perfect forms of play' (Huzinga). Dance enables us to move from being simply a spectator of the game to a participant in the game itself. I have always found the greatest release in worship of God when I have had the freedom to dance. Whenever the Bible calls us to 'Rejoice in the Lord!' this is actually an invitation to dance!

Finally, Pastor Suurmond explains that charismatic celebration is like play because it is ' "different" from "ordinary life" '. It takes no great leap of the imagination to translate 'different' as holy and it should not be seen as unusual that 're-creation' should take place on a holy day (holiday). Because the kingdom of God is 'among us' but also 'coming', it intersects the natural world so that the church and the celebration is *in* the world but not *of* the world. Sadly, our services and our celebrations have tended to forget this. They have become more like battlegrounds than playgrounds where, instead of wrestling principalities, we fight one another. Because celebration has lost the element of play it has also lost its capacity to transform. Instead of telling stories, as Jesus did, we tend to moralise. Instead of truly worshipping, we seek to be "relevant" and so become little different from the world. Is it any wonder that many of our institutional churches no longer attract worshippers? The celebration has ceased to be inspirational. 'The celebration is no longer foolish enough, so that it no longer proclaims God's wisdom' (Suurmond).

Play has much to teach us about worship. I do hope that all the above didn't seem too theological, particularly after all I've said before. These are, after all, just foolish thoughts. Descartes may well have said *'cogito, ergo sum'* but I say *'ludo ergo sum'* – so there! You don't have to be a clown to understand this, but if you are it helps!

As children we waste our days in playgrounds and parks, idling away the hours in joyful recreation. Clowns and circuses, stories and games, fun and fancy and laughter: all these liberate and humanise us. When we grow up we tend to forget the fun of trailing a balloon on brightly coloured string. We exchange our playing fields for battlefields and our parks for offices. Our play, and our worship, becomes too much like our work, and we push it to have relevance and meaning. Yet, if we take the time to stop and look, the rollercoasters and roundabouts, the seesaws and swings and slides are there waiting for us to learn from them again. King David only asked God for one thing – that he might dwell in God's house, gaze on his beauty and seek him in his temple.

I think that's where I'd like to play too.

If I had my life to live over, I would relax more.
I wouldn't take so many things so seriously.
I would take more chances.
I would climb more mountains, and swim more rivers . . .
Next time I'd start barefooted earlier in the spring
And stay that way later in the fall.
I wouldn't make such good grades unless I enjoyed working for them.
I'd go to more dances.
I'd ride on more merry-go-rounds.
I'd pick more daisies.

Frank Dickey (or Nadine Stair)

One thing is needful
(Luke 10)

Rest

What we need to do

'We are becoming increasingly restless.'
Anthony Gormley (Architect: *Angel of the North*)

'Come with me by yourselves to a quiet
place and get some rest.'
Jesus (Mark 6:31)

13

FIRST BREATH:
HOLIDAYS

And so we come to the last section of foolish reflections: on the subject of Rest. I've included it last
because it is unquestionably the most important
and probably the most misunderstood. In the
phrase 'Work, Rest and Play' it sits between the
other two not in order to please chocolate bar manufacturers but because it is this part of our lives
that keeps the other two in harmony and balance.

If the title were a seesaw Work and Play would
be two children sitting on opposite seats. Rest
would be perfectly poised in the middle – an equi-
distant counterbalance. Rightly understood it
quickens and enables both our work and our play,
protecting the former from monotony and stress
and the latter from child*ish*ness and banality. It is
greatly undervalued because it is seen as non-pro-
ductive. It is usually synonymous with a word that
comes at the end of a list, as in 'and the rest'. It
becomes a kind of glorified etcetera. In reality, it is
a fundamental key to improving the quality of life
and a theological truth as foundational as creation
itself.

Restful or Restless?

The word 'Rest' is interesting in itself. It could be seen as comprising two abbreviations: 're' being short for regarding and 'st' an abbreviation of saint. I don't think it stretches the credulity too much to say Rest could therefore be concerning that which is holy. For rest is indeed a most holy thing we would do well to incorporate fully into our lives. The word holy (Gk. *hagion*) means 'set apart' or 'devoted to' so that a holy day is one that is different from the others. We should not think it strange then that a holy day should become a holiday; that is, a time of rest and recreation, distinct from a day usually given over to work, eating and sleep. Sadly, holidays are seen as a kind of reward offered for having done sufficient work. Many people defer taking holidays as though this were a kind of virtue. The excuses given are usually lack of money or time or pressure of work. People who do not take frequent holidays or who manage with less rest are held up as paragons to be admired.

We have clearly lived for some time in a society where useful and gainful employment is a high aspiration and doing nothing is considered idleness. Being able to manage with less sleep and working seven days a week with hardly any time off is seen at best as a necessary evil and at worst as a noble and admirable characteristic. Rest has indeed become a four-letter word. We have become so concerned with being seen as industrious and hard working that we anxiously try to impress others with how busy we are. Consider the following scenarios:

We meet a friend or business colleague on the train. They ask, 'How's it going? Busy?' We reply,

'Oh, yes! Rushed off my feet! Scarcely a minute to sit down! Hardly a moment to myself!' We *never* say, 'Oh no, I'm hardly doing a thing at the moment. Nice and relaxed. Got my feet up most of the time!' The reason is that the former response is probably true. But even if it weren't, would we dare admit it?

The phone rings at 9.30 am on a Saturday morning. We're snoozing in bed. It's a day off and we're having a lie-in. We jump up, rubbing the sleep out of our eyes and stumble to the phone. A voice asks, 'Sorry to disturb you (chuckle). I didn't get you out of bed did I?' We reply, 'Oh no, not at all! You know me – up with the lark!' We *daren't* admit we were resting. Others get up early, why shouldn't we? But how do we know our friend on the phone is not calling from his or her own bed?

We're staying at a friend's for a few days. We get up late one morning, missing breakfast. As we enter the kitchen to make a coffee our friend says brightly, with not a little trace of sarcasm, 'Good *afternoon!*' We look sheepish, we feel guilty; we can't possibly excuse the sin of having overslept!

When I was a youngster I loved to go camping with the scouts. I went right through the movement, achieving Queen Scout status, and had the great pleasure of taking my own son camping. I well remember, beyond all the badges and awards I sewed on my uniform, the supreme accolade was always being the first up in the morning. A kind of invisible aura always clung to the one who could rise before all the others, build and light the fire, heat a dixie of water and make themselves a cup of tea! An air of beneficent supremacy attached to the one who could greet the sticky-eyed faces peering

through the tent flap with a gracious and self-satis-
fied smile that proclaimed: 'I don't need to rest as
long as you guys; I'm made of sterner stuff!'

When we were very young we hated going to
bed early because it underlined the fact that we
were inferior juveniles. We needed to rest because
we were young and we didn't understand. When
we were naughty we were sent to our bedrooms so
they often became places associated with punish-
ment. Even when we grew older we liked to stop
out late, eschewing rest and sleep as though they
were imposters or weaknesses for lesser mortals.
Even now the one who stays up longest or who
rises earliest (and preferably both) somehow has
the edge: a kind of enhanced moral authority.

Restless Vicars

Once again, I say to my shame, the clergy are in the
vanguard of this fear of rest and veneration of
work and busyness. Yes, they're right up there with
junior doctors, farmers, commodities brokers and a
host of other workaholics. Revd. So-and-So complains bitterly that he hasn't had a day off in
months, he's up to his neck in weddings and funerals, his in-tray is two foot high and the Bishop's just
asked him to take on another committee! And the
rest of us cluck sympathetically and commiserate.
We know what it's like. Some of us try to top the
complaining priest. We're working harder and
we've gone even longer without a day off. *And*
without a proper holiday! It's a kind of badge we
wear that says work is good and rest is bad.

It's no surprise that a major contributor to
breakdown of clergy marriage is the 'other
woman'. I refer of course, to the church. But it's not

the organisation itself that inputs the stress any more than the bank makes the manager work hard. It's what we do with the job; the way we treat it that gets away with us. If the baptisms, weddings, funerals and Communions weren't there, many clergy would find other things to keep them busy because a busy priest is a good priest, a real priest, an authentic priest. And, despite their complaints, many of them welcome it and continue to shun the need for rest. And hundreds of clergy, when they retire find themselves working just as hard, if not harder, helping out in various parishes and on sundry boards and committees. Even having the so-called 'choice' to rest, they take the option of more and more work.

I suppose these criticisms could be equally applied to a score of other professions and conditions. I speak of what I know and I don't exclude myself. Even clowns forget to play and refuse to rest and this clown is no exception!

Having caricatured the attitude that says work is good and rest is bad I don't want you to think I'm suggesting we blindly adopt the opposite position. Work is good and rest is good also but both need to be understood and rightly balanced. The opposite of a workaholic is a couch potato and there is neither refreshment nor holiness in that. Our problem is that the pendulum has swung too far towards work: the seesaw has tipped up in favour of frenetic activity and Rest lies all bemired in the mud. The result is pressure and stress and reliance on only one area of life to give us meaning and authentication. This was never supposed to be. What enjoyment can be gained from an immobile seesaw?

Like a child on a seesaw or a man on a bike or a clown on a slack rope we need periodically to adjust our balance. This will provide enjoyment as well as direction. We were not intended to spend our entire lives asleep nor entertaining ourselves, but neither were we intended to spend them all constantly working. Nowadays, our culture insists that we work because we have to be productive. Everybody is expected to 'do their bit'. Rest is reinterpreted as sloth and we are made to feel guilty if we take too much of it. Consequently, we tend to break not only the fourth commandment, but the first and second as well. Work becomes an idol, a 'false god' that we can so easily elevate above all else. The Mennonite author Doris Longacre, quoted in *Margin* writes:

> Profit-making work began to swallow Sundays and holidays. No wonder everyone has been getting so tired.
>
> Obviously much of this fatigue takes place in the name of making more money, even though the pantry's already stocked. After all, by burning a little more gas and working one more evening a week, it is possible to chase down one more account, open another store, or farm another field. But it may not be possible to love a spouse, children, and the friendless poor at the same time.[1]

A very great number of the ills of our society could be traced back to an absence of true rest. In constructing his huge statue *The Angel of the North*, outside Gateshead, the architect Anthony Gormley observed that 'we live in an increasingly restless society'. Whatever we may think of modern architecture, we can applaud the sentiments of those who seek to draw us into the silent contemplation of something whose purpose is not to provide shelter or an environment in which to work but rather to give us opportunity to rest. The great cathedral architects of the past knew also what it was to build a structure for contemplation, squandering size and space to convey the awesome majesty of God; creating something where the soul might find rest.

Why not sit back now and make some time and space to read this last section in peace. Better still, take an hour or two off before you read it and do nothing at all . . . OK? Now take a long cool drink or a nice hot cuppa and a couple of your favourite biscuits and relax in an easy chair. Take six deep breaths. Are you sitting comfortably? Then you can continue. We start with a real hot potato. The Sabbath!

14

SECOND BREATH: KEEPING THE SABBATH

Picture the scene: Mum stands at the foot of the stairs and calls up in a loud voice: 'Hurry up! It's Sunday and you've got to go to church!' Back comes the answer: 'I'm not going!' 'Why not?' 'I'll give you two reasons. One: I don't like anyone in that church! Two: nobody in that church likes me!' Mother swiftly replies: 'I'll give you two reasons why you *are* going! One: you're forty-three years of age. Two: you're the vicar!'

Sundays

For many vicars (pastors, priests, ministers etc.) Sunday can be the least holy day of the week. Surveys show it can be the most stressful, least restful time of all for those who are called to lead congregations, read lessons, conduct the intercessions, hand out the books, play the organ etc. Monday blues and the 'post Easter slump' are common enough factors amongst the clergy. But does it have to be like this?

When we start to consider the concept of the Holy Day we will inevitably turn to the Sabbath. Jurgen Moltmann said that it was the Sabbath, not man that was the crown of God's creation, for it was made after man. Jesus said: 'The Sabbath was made for man, not man for the Sabbath' (Mark 2:27). However, not content with trying to fashion God in our own image, we seem to be trying to make the Sabbath fit our own preconceived criteria as well. In this vitally important area we face some huge misconceptions – so convoluted in fact, that we need to deal with them one by one.

Misconception number one: the Sabbath and the Lord's Day are one and the same. Everything in the Bible that refers to the Sabbath can also be applied to Sunday. **This is not true.** Now, I'm not having a go at the Lord's Day Observance Society or denigrating the Keep Sunday Special Campaign. I believe Sunday is a special and holy day and that we should observe it. But let's not get it confused with the Sabbath. Sunday is clearly the first day of the week; the day God created the light, the day the Son rose, the day the Spirit came. John 20 verse 1 tells us the day of Resurrection was 'the first day of the week'. After Jesus ascended to heaven the disciples marked the first day of the week as a day distinct from Sabbath, when they remembered the Resurrection and worshipped the risen Christ. It has rightly lasted until now as the special day on which all Christians gather to fellowship together and offer their praises to Almighty God. It is referred to as a Day of Rest and many people try to observe it as a day that is different from others. Many do not go to work on that day; some will spend time with their family, wash the car or mow the lawn. Christians will 'go to church'. Many countries, whose laws are based on a biblical value system, curtail the amount and type of trading that takes place on a Sunday and legislate to preserve the distinctiveness of that day from others. All this is good. But 'Sunday' is not the same as 'Sabbath'. It is only part of the story.

Misconception number two: Sabbath is intrinsically Jewish and can be only understood in that context. The Sabbath day is the seventh day. *'Shabat'* means 'seventh'. In this country it is called Saturday, in Italy: Sabbato. Sabbath has been celebrated by the Jews since its inception in the book of Exodus.

> This is what the LORD commanded: 'Tomorrow is to be a day of rest, a holy Sabbath to the LORD.'
> (Exodus 16:23)

In the same way that Christians celebrate Sunday as their Holy Day and Muslims keep Friday as their Holy Day, so Jews keep the Sabbath, the seventh day of the week. Professor David Ford tells of a rabbi being asked on television how the Jews had managed to preserve the Sabbath for thousands of years. His reply was: 'It is not the Jews who have preserved the Sabbath. The Sabbath has preserved the Jews.'[1]

In a religion so firmly based on the family the Sabbath has had a profound effect. It has indeed preserved the Jews and much that they hold dear about their faith. It has established rest and holiness much more securely in their paradigm than it has for Western Christendom. But the Sabbath is *not* just for the Jews.

Sabbath and Sunday are *not* the same. The most that can be said is that Sunday can be *a* Sabbath but not *the* Sabbath. The principle of Sabbath is much wider and deeper, as we shall see in a moment.

Misconception number three: the Sabbath is to be seen only in terms of a particular day to be kept holy and distinct. It would seem from the fourth commandment that this exactly what God is commanding his people.

> 'Remember the Sabbath day by keeping it holy. Six days you shall labour and do all your work; but the seventh day is a Sabbath to the LORD your God.'
>
> (Exodus 20:8–10)

This does appear to state that it is only the seventh day; the Saturday (or whatever we may wish to call it) is to be kept as Sabbath. If this were truly the case then to keep it on another day, such as Sunday or Friday, would be breaking one of the Ten Commandments. Or if you believe that the fourth command was superseded by the new covenant and the Sabbath day changed to a Sunday to coincide with the Resurrection festival then to keep any other time is also to disobey God.

If that is the case. But I believe it is not. Bear in mind the passage says the seventh day is *a* Sabbath. Clearly the first day may be a Sabbath also, or the fifth, or the third. To tie down the Sabbath only to a particular day is to entirely miss the principle that God is seeking to impart to his people. To work feverishly for six days in order to squeeze in our Sabbath on Saturday or Sunday is to fail to grasp what the Lord God is trying to teach us about Rest and Holiness. It is not something we earn as a bonus nor yet something we slavishly follow as a regulation. It is a principle for life. Our days and weeks and years should be filled with holy

Sabbaths, rightly placed as counterpoints to work and play. It is good for Christians (and for Jews and Muslims) to have a day that most can join in together. It will rightly be a holy day, a day of rest, of worship and of celebration. It will be a day that is set apart as different. But Sabbath is not solely that. God teaches us to Sabbath as an antidote to busyness, even as tithing is an antidote to materialism. The principle is that we set aside a seventh of our time to be a Still Time, to be a holy Sabbath.

Final (and worst) misconception: the Sabbath is a religious idea that does not have central importance. Although keeping the Sabbath is one of the Big Ten it shouldn't usually rate with the major theological themes of Repentance, the Atonement, the Incarnation, Original Sin and so on. **Wrong!**

Sabbath is of the utmost importance. Without it we are lost; condemned to a restless and unholy religion, bereft of meaning and aching for true life. God never intended that Sabbath should be bundled up inside mere 'religion'; it is something he has built into the very fabric of life. The Sabbath is not actually mentioned first in Exodus 16 at all. It goes right back to the dawn of time. When God made people on Day Six it was so they could enjoy a Sabbath holiday as their first day. They had done nothing to earn it; it was a free gift. When God rested on the seventh day it wasn't because he was tired. The Lord of All was setting an example. He was modelling Sabbath, demonstrating a principle for his new creation.

It is because we fail to see the true significance of Sabbath that we miss so many blessings and hit so many pitfalls. And once again it seems that the worst offenders are the dear old clergy. We break the fourth commandment week after week. Granted, we have to work on Sundays: our 'busy day', so we're told. (If someone else says to me 'Of course, you only work Sundays, don't you?' I may just break the sixth commandment!) For many, that seems to let us off having any kind of 'day off'. For most it's a bit of a joke, an old chestnut that crops up again and again at clergy gatherings. 'We wish we had time,' we say, 'but there's so much to do.' Actually, we commit a terrible sin, against God and against ourselves, as destructive in its way as lying, stealing or blasphemy, for it contains elements of all three. For six days we engage in work, tasks that seek to achieve something. The seventh day is intended to be different; a time when we remember it is not work that saves us but God's grace.

Breaking the Sabbath

If we ever think that breaking the Sabbath is a minor offence we should consider the difficult passage in Numbers 15. Here a man gathering sticks on the Sabbath is brought before Moses and Aaron. The Lord commands that he is executed and the Israelites stone him to death. This is one of those stories we wish were not in the Bible. It seems so unfair that a man die for such a small infringement. For all we know he could have been collecting firewood for his family: what about his dependants after this terrible event? We can only speculate on the circumstances surrounding this story and be horrified by the starkness and suddenness of this death. What we can know for sure, is that breaking the Sabbath was no minor infringement to be excused or laughed off. It was serious, deadly serious. The Ten Commandments were not some 'good idea' that could be lightly set aside. God taught the foundational principles of life to his children as Law, so that under Grace they might become mature, accepting the principles as habitual constituents of everyday living. Honouring God, respect for parents, protection of interpersonal relationships by upholding truth and integrity – the sanctity of marriage and of life itself, and keeping the Sabbath. This was the stuff of life and it was not just to be learned and obeyed; it was to become ingrained in society. Nowadays, we don't stone people for breaking the Sabbath, or telling lies, or dishonouring the Name of God but this does not mean they are not to be taken deadly seriously. As a people living under God's grace, these principles should be habits: part of the very fabric of life.

Failure to understand the importance of the Sabbath may yet be our undoing. Seeing it as something of small consequence, an 'extra' we observe if we have the time, is a most serious mistake. Without Sabbath in our lives, we undermine the benefits of the cross and delay the advent of true revival. With it, we may even see the vicar at the beginning of this chapter looking forward to Sundays!

Great blessings await those who will set their hearts to truly keep the Sabbath.

'If you keep your feet from breaking the Sabbath and from doing as you please on my holy day, if you call the Sabbath a delight and the LORD's holy day honourable, and if you honour it by not going your own way and not doing as you please or speaking idle words, then you will find your joy in the LORD, and I will cause you to ride on the heights of the land and to feast on the inheritance of your father Jacob.' The mouth of the LORD has spoken.

(Isaiah 58:13, 14)

15

THIRD BREATH:
LESSONS FROM THE EXODUS

What do you do when you've been given responsibility for looking after two million people? You're not as young as you were (over eighty in this case) and you need to lead them through a hostile wilderness without any real provision for food and water. In addition, despite the fact that you've just had a pretty spectacular deliverance from your former oppressors, a lot of your charges are starting to grumble and complain and are comparing their present condition rather less favourably with their former slavery. What do you do? You do what Moses often did when facing these kinds of problems. He used the well tried arrow prayer many of us use when we desperately need God: 'HELP!'

Manna and Quail

God responded by providing his people with manna (a type of honey-flavoured wafer bread) and quails (a sort of short-tailed migratory bird like a small partridge), and also by instigating the Sabbath. You can read about this in Exodus 16 and find further details of Sabbath regulations in Deuteronomy 5. Some very valuable lessons can be learned from a close study of these two passages.

First of all, it is fascinating to note that God provides not only for the immediate physical needs of his people, but far more importantly, for their social and spiritual needs as well. The bread and the birds feed their bodies but the Sabbath feeds their souls. God tells them that the Sabbath is to be a holy day (holiday), a day of rest on which they will do no work. That means no tent-repairing, no digging or carpentry, no cooking . . . and no collecting of manna and quails. In fact there would be no provision of manna and quails at all on the Sabbath. God would provide twice as much the day before and the people were to collect for two days. The manna would not go rotten overnight and it would remain fresh to be eaten on the Sabbath. God entirely removed the need for work. Of course, some people went out on the Sabbath anyway, to see if there was any food and some people collected extra on days other than the one before Sabbath, even though they'd been told not to. (Some things never change!) There was no manna and quails on Sabbath and the manna kept over on other days went maggoty and smelly.

For forty years this miraculous provision persisted. For six days the Israelites worked, harvesting quail in the evening and collecting manna in the morning. And on Sabbath they rested. Moses told them clearly that God provided extra the day before so that they could enjoy the rest that he had given them on the Sabbath. Rest was given to all: man, woman and child. In addition work was provided for all, regardless of experience and ability.

The Israelites did as they were told; some gathered much, some little. And when they measured it by the omer, he who gathered much did not have too much, and he who gathered little did not have too little. Each one gathered as much as he needed.

(Exodus 16:17, 18)

God always provides as much as we need. The pattern in Exodus 16 shows us a God who offers his people a harmonious existence, rightly balancing work and rest and enabling all to participate. The Israelites are neither unemployed or over-employed. They are unable to hoard the product of their work but are encouraged to be dependent on God each day. There are surely some lessons to be learned for us, living in the stress-bound techno-driven world at the dawning of the twentieth-first century. Purpose-guided labour for all that are willing to work, dependence on a loving God and appreciation of Sabbath: these are the kind of values that could revitalise society.

It may be that many of Moses' followers questioned the institution of Sabbath and wondered at its importance. Nowadays there are a number that cannot understand the need for regular breaks between work and see no value in taking time off. In Deuteronomy 5 God sets out four reasons for resting and keeping holy the Sabbath. They may be summarised under the headings: Review, Reverence, Relax and Remember.

Review, Reverence, Relax and Remember

Resting is important because it gives us the opportunity to *review* what we've achieved. At times it becomes necessary to step aside from our activities and evaluate. God himself sets the precedent in

creation through work, observation and evaluation. He spoke and it came to be (work); he saw
(observation) and it was good (evaluation). God
took a moment at the end of each day to examine
what he'd made and attach value to it. 'And God
saw that it was good' (Genesis 1:10). Rest gives us
the chance to examine what has gone before, to
take stock and assess. Too little time is allowed in
our schedules for this and we find ourselves rushing from task to task without the opportunity to
appreciate the value of what we have already done.
We are to 'observe' the Sabbath (Deuteron-omy
5:12) and so review the progress of our lives.

Rest gives us the opportunity to *revere* that
which God has set aside as holy. In Jeremiah 17
God's people are reminded not to carry loads on
the Sabbath and Ezekiel 20 says God was angry at
the people's disobedience and because 'they utterly desecrated my Sabbaths'. We are little better
today. Not only do we fill our lives with restless-
ness, but also we can make our Sabbaths just as
busy as any other day. When we need to be setting
apart time as holy we actually load one another
down with extra burdens we were commanded not
to carry. When we crowd out rest time or fill that
which we've set aside as distinct, we are just as
guilty of Sabbath desecration as those early Jews.
We are not just to 'keep' the Sabbath; we are to
'keep it holy'.

Rest gives us simply the opportunity to *relax*.
'Relax. Don't do it!' was the simple motto which
became the words of a popular song a few years
ago. We are very much part of a society which finds
it hard to do nothing. We have relaxation tech-
niques and relaxation classes and relaxation tapes

of wind and dolphins and birdsong. Few doubt the value of relaxation but many find it illusive. Retreats and quiet days abound but they are still seen as extraordinary and not something that should be a part of life. It is clear we need to learn when to stop working and be still. There is nothing wrong with doing nothing and just 'being' for a while! Taking the chance to switch off the constant inflow of information for a moment and just listening to the rhythm of our hearts will provide enormous soul refreshment. In Exodus 31 verse 17 we are reminded that God himself 'abstained from work and rested'. Work is to be renounced on the Sabbath (Deuteronomy 5:13), not because it is bad, but because it can so easily get out of hand. Work can become a seductive idol we worship just as easily as money, fame or beauty. As it threatens to overwhelm us we must cry: 'Peace! Be still!' and embrace the calm. Relaxation is a vital part of Sabbath. If we rest we will be blessed!

Finally, rest gives us an opportunity to *remember*. Verse 15 of Deuteronomy 5 tells us to: 'Remember that you were slaves in Egypt and that the LORD your God brought you out of there . . .' The great festival of Pesach encourages the Jewish people to recall, and symbolically re-enact, the drama of the exodus through a family meal. Sabbath shows we who were slaves are now free. We have free will. We can *choose* to rest! For the Christian Egypt symbolises the slavery of sin and the exodus shows the picture of the journey of faith. Having got out of Egypt, the Israelites 'acted out' the drama of the Sabbath for forty years in the wilderness in order to get Egypt out of them. We *were* slaves, but we are slaves no longer. God has brought us out of the

'have to' realm of guilt and busyness into the freedom of Sabbath. We must remember that.
Everyone needs a Sabbath. No one should be
forced to work seven days a week, either by their
own addiction or the compulsion of an employer. If
this is the case then we become slaves, either to our
own fears and drives or to the will of another. The
particular value of campaigns like 'Keep Sunday
Special' is that it stands against the drive to press
thousands into modern day slavery by forcing
them to work when they need to rest. We were
slaves. We are no longer. God commands us to
remember that.

Rest in the Rhythm of Life

Rest is vital for well being and is built into life from
the beginning. The huge muscle thumping away
non-stop inside our chests (we hope!) is designed
to rest between every beat. In nature certain ani-
mals take out several months of the year to rest and
we've all seen what happens to Yogi Bear when his
hibernation is disturbed! Rest is seen in the rhythm
of the seasons: the slow decline of autumn and
'death' of winter, turning to the 'new birth' of
spring and blossoming of summer. If we have eyes
to see, the principles of Rest are all around us.
Matter and time are part of the creation that God
has called us to subdue. We are to be the masters
not the slaves, but we are called to a discipline of
balance that will include rest as part of the great
cycle of life.

The lesson is unquestionably hard to learn.
Forty years of travel in the wilderness were not sufficient to impart it fully. God's patient whisper still
calls to us: 'Be still and know . . .' Like rebellious

children or an inconstant lover we must be wooed back to God's embrace. Hiding, like Adam in the garden of delight, God comes looking for us again to teach us once more the lessons of Life.

Many years ago, following a long session of illness, I complained to an old and wise Christian friend that I was getting so little done and all this enforced inactivity was so frustrating. 'Ah!' she said, smiling knowingly and quoting her favourite psalm. 'He *makes* me lie down in green pastures . . .'

'He *makes* me lie down . . .', I don't think I would make myself do it. As I have waited in weakness to see the promises of God fulfilled and still wait, often frustrated and impatient, I remember that God waits also for me. In his waiting room he prepares me and strengthens me and reassures me before he calls me. As we kick and struggle against the call to rest and cling fondly to the idols of industry, the heavenly Father sometimes *makes* us lie down. You don't have to be a clown to understand this, but if you are it helps!

Traffic Lights

In my first parish where I initially contracted the virus that led to my ME there is a set of traffic lights in the centre of the town. Incredibly, from whichever direction I approached they were always red and I had to wait. Perhaps, even then, God was teaching me the value of waiting and the Sabbath rest.

Sometimes traffic lights are green and you must go. You must move on in the journey, like the Israelites following the pillar of cloud and fire in the desert, going where God calls you, when he calls you. When the light is green you don't want to hang around kicking your heels, looking back to what used to be, unwilling to move forward. Green means go for it!

When the light is amber that means you are to get ready. Look in the mirror; remember where you've been. Check your position in the car and on the road; make sure your seatbelt is secure. Prepare to select the correct gear and position your foot near the accelerator. Put your hand by the brake but don't release it yet. Keep still but get ready! Any moment now there will be a green light and you will be able to go, but not yet! The time is not right at the moment. This is a preparation time, a time for getting ready. If you don't take the appropriate actions now, when the light changes you won't be ready and you'll miss out. So get ready!

When the light is red that means wait. Don't switch the engine off! Don't get out of the car and walk home! Don't unpack your picnic hamper and get the squash and sandwiches out! Do wait. And watch. And keep your eye on those lights because sometime, sooner or later, they're going to change. But for now – sit still and wait!

My churchwarden Bob (who is a highly efficient police officer) has asked me to point out, in the interests of Road Safety, that amber means nothing *except* wait! So if, perchance, you should find yourself stuck at those lights on either red or amber you might like to think about dear old Moses and the aptly named *children* of Israel. They all had to keep their eyes fixed on the right thing and, in Review, Reverence, Relaxation and Remembrance, know when to move on and when to wait.

16

FOURTH BREATH:
LESSONS FROM JOSHUA

Not long ago I was at a Christian Leaders' conference when there was a call for those desiring 'ministry' to come out to the front. Feeling an inner
prompting I duly left my seat and joined the queue
of ministers waiting to be prayed for. As I stood in
line I clearly heard that inner voice tell me to take
off my shoes and wait where I was! I obeyed, feeling rather foolish, but expecting that I would be
approached by someone with a life-changing message or great words of wisdom for me. After about
half an hour (by which time I was feeling a bit
cheesed off) the little voice, which I knew to be the
Holy Sprit, told me to go back to my seat.

'Well, God!' I stormed inwardly as I sat down
and replaced my shoes. 'What was all that about? I
waited; where was the message?'

'That was it,' he replied. 'Just wait.'

I must confess I didn't jump up and down with
delight at either the wisdom or humour of God. It
took me some time to face up to my disappointment but, after a while, I knew he was right. I
reflected upon the fact that, over the years, the one
thing God has spoken to me about over and over

again, in Word, prophecy and symbol, is the need to wait.

Good Things for Those who Wait

The latest Guinness advertisement has an old Mediterranean guy called Marco racing against his barman pulling a pint. The slogan is *'Good things come to those who wait'*. Scarcely was a truer word spoken. Waiting is a forgotten art. We live in the 'now' generation who want it yesterday. They tell me that in America it's not worth marrying someone unless they can prepare you a meal in less than half an hour! You're not 'waited on' in the fast food establishments any more. There isn't time! Most of the new hamburger outlets being built today are 'drive-thru' so you don't even need to park the car. Talk as fast as you can to a mechanical grill, throw your money through a window, grab your burger at the next and it's 'Have a nice daaayy!' You're off! Why wait? Some credit card advertisements have the slogan, 'Taking the waiting out of wanting!' Having had the usual bad experiences of credit cards – take my advice: it's better to wait!

Two months in the US and Canada gave me ample opportunity to observe patience in airport departure lounges. Most people are frantic to *do* something. They pace up and down, read newspapers and books, look repeatedly out of the windows or make numerous trips to the restroom (why do they call it that?). Finally, when the announcer calls: 'We are now pre-boarding families with young children, executive-class passengers and those needing special assistance', everybody makes a mad dash for the doors to board the aircraft! Let's face it, we all hate waiting.

Think how we chafe in the doctor or dentist's surgery, at the supermarket checkout, or in that interminable traffic jam. We repeatedly consult our watches, mutter under our breath, get more and more tense and occasionally burst out with a very Victor Meldrew-like 'Oh no! I do not believe it!' Most of us (in the Western world, at least) find it very difficult to wait for anything. We're like the prayer I saw on a tea towel once: 'Lord, give me patience. And I want it NOW!' It's all very unlike the relaxed attitude to organisation you'll find in places like Africa. They do say the English got the watches and the Africans got the time! You may find a high level of poverty and deprivation in many developing countries but you will also find a high level of patience and a much greater willingness to wait. Could that be one of the reasons the Church there is growing so quickly?

Waiting is considered to be unproductive because it is seen by many as empty and valueless. It appears to be a waste of time. Yet, if time has been created to serve us, then waiting is only another assertion of our mastery. If time is to be our servant, why are we so concerned about wasting it? There are occasions when time should be squandered, if only to emphasise that we are in control, just as it is sometimes important to be liberal in our giving in order to dethrone the idol of mammon. Waiting need not be unproductive at all, even if it appears empty. Many professions rely on waiting to achieve a result: wine making for example, or maturing a cheese or a fine spirit. In nature there are many things that improve with waiting, for the experience is part of the rhythm of life.

See how the farmer waits for the land to yield its valuable crop and how patient he is for the autumn and spring rains. You too, be patient and stand firm . . .

(James 5:7, 8)

The industrial and technological revolutions have brought us many good things but they have done nothing for our patience. Machines demand our attention immediately and 'beep' at us if we are tardy. The speed and complexity of communication technology somehow invades our spirits and gobbles up our stillness. One of my congregation remarked to me recently that life felt like you were rushing along so fast that when you 'jumped off' there was a great sense of inertia, with people and things continuing to rush past you.

Airports and Canals

A short time ago I had the opportunity, with my wife, Kim, to spend a weekend on a narrow boat with my churchwarden and his wife. Just a few hours prior to beginning this experience I had been in Los Angeles International Airport with crowds of holidaymakers returning to Britain or starting their vacation. The contrast could hardly have been starker. From an environment of heat, noise and chaos, surrounded by hundreds of people and masses of technology, I was transferred to a world of peace and tranquillity, to be shared with three special friends, a few moorhens and the beauty of nature. It seemed that at one moment I was crammed into the seat of a Virgin 747 and the next stretched out lazily in the spacious surroundings of a fifty-foot canal boat. I exchanged the babble of tourists and the roar of jet engines for the sweet song of river birds and the 'phut phut' of a small inboard motor. The peace and stillness of the Grand Union canal on a Sunday morning in late August has to be experienced to be believed. What an incredible experience it is to gaze across a mirrored water surface, broken only by the wake of a coot or to drift gently along a bank, watching intently for the sudden electric blue of a kingfisher and to be enfolded in the utter fathomless quiet of unspoilt countryside. 'It's life, Jim, but not as we know it!'

Not all of us are able to experience the wonders of canal cruising and, even if we are, there are times when we must return to airport terminals and offices and shops and homes. We can't stay on the mountaintop when we are called to live in the valley. Even though it is harder to wait there, sometimes the returns are even more valuable. In the eye of the storm there is a still place and it is the contrast of the waiting with the rush that can make the former even more precious, for it can provide the resources we need to confidently enter the storm again. Waiting enables us to hear God and to be prepared to respond to his call.

Waiting at Gilgal

In the book of Joshua the narrative of the exodus from Egypt turns from wandering in the wilderness to entry into the Promised Land. The Israelites had been obliged to wait before they could receive what God had promised them in Canaan. Now, at last they stand on the very borders of the place they had been dreaming about for so long. The land 'flowing with milk and honey', that Moses had spoken of and their parents brought them up on,

was at last to be theirs. It would be understandable
that they felt a little impatient as they awaited the
report of the small surveillance party that went
ahead of them. Admittedly, the great Moses was no
more but in Joshua, son of Nun, Moses' foremost
disciple, they had a formidable leader. Joshua had
been with them since they left Egypt and he was
now the only one, save Caleb, who remembered
those days. Joshua, the great military commander,
full of the power of God and schooled in the wisdom of Moses the Lawgiver, would now swiftly
lead them to possess the land of Canaan. The book
of Joshua opens with God speaking to Joshua,
telling him he will be with him just as he was with
Moses. He gives Joshua many promises and
encouragements. Then Joshua leads the nation of
Israel across the Jordan, a miracle as momentous in
its way as the crossing of the Red Sea. Everyone is
very upbeat and positive. The army is keen to rush
in and take the territory! But there are still two
important lessons to learn and they are both to do
with waiting. They are Gilgal and Jericho.

When the Israelites cross the Jordan they camp
on the further bank at a place called Gilgal and
Joshua commands that twelve stones that had been
taken from the bed of the river be set up as a testi-
mony to the power and provision of God. Waiting
and resting almost always give us opportunities to
remember what God has done for us.

Now, Joshua's new army is keen to advance and
the people are eager to see God's promises fulfilled. The Canaanites are afraid of them and every
indication is that they will surrender in the face of
a people whose God can do miracles (Joshua 5:1).
Is there really any need to wait further? Let's imag-

ine the scene in the tent of Field Marshall Joshua as his officers come to discuss their battle plans.

The air is thick with the smell of goat hair and the smoke of the lamps as the young generals gather around Joshua's table. Yet there is an unmistakable atmosphere of excitement. After all the years of wandering, all the planning, and all the dreams, at last: action! In the encampment outside forty thousand men are ready and eager to fight! Zerah scratches his beard and ventures his first suggestion.

'Well, Joshua. Here's how I see it. Jericho is a powerful city but its people are scared of us. How about a diversion to lure them out onto the plain where we can easily defeat them?'

Ephraim is not so sure. 'I think a siege is the answer,' he ventures gruffly. 'Caleb and his boys come in from the west and sweep the walls with volleys of arrows whilst Asher leads in the siege towers to the east side and my company rams the main gate!'

'It's a frontal attack we need!' shouts Baruch. 'Forget the siege towers and scaling ladders. Waste of time! Listen – we tunnel in through here.' He stabs a finger at the roughly drawn parchment in front of him.

And so the arguments range back and forth as each general excitedly puts forward his own plans for the best attack. Meanwhile, Joshua sits smiling behind his desk. Finally, he holds up his hand for silence. The young generals look up from their sketch maps and the lines and squares they've made in the dust. What will their great leader say?

'That's *not* what we're going to do. God has another plan.'

'But Joshua,' interrupts Ephraim. 'You can't mean . . . hang on! What are you doing with that flint knife . . .?!!'

Given the favourable circumstances and the high morale of his men, any ordinary army commander would have swept in and put Jericho to the sword immediately. But Joshua wasn't an ordinary commander. He was a man who listened to God. On the banks of the Jordan, in the very shadow of Jericho, when every circumstance and every man seemed to be saying, 'Go!' Joshua disabled his entire army.

He circumcised every mother's son of them!

In pain and discomfort they were made to wait until they were healed and until God gave them the command to go. Here at last, on the fourteenth day of the month, God took the last vestiges of Egypt out of his people and for the first time since leaving Egypt they celebrated the Passover. The next day they ate produce from Canaan and the manna and quail they'd had for forty years ceased. When every other instinct and indication told them to go, they waited.

It's hard to wait when all you've dreamed of seems just round the next bend. Everything is going so well and then there's a setback, an obstacle that causes you to wait. More often than not it's something uncomfortable or distressing. Yet the promises of God are frequently claimed through weakness. We have to wait simply because that thing we were so eager to grab is not yet ready for us. And God wants us to know that it is his sovereign power, not our ability or experience, that has brought us to where we are. Waiting humbles us; it makes us dependent. There are things we have carried with us that need to be left in the waiting room. As we wait, God will cut those things away and prepare us for what is to come.

Waiting at Jericho

Even when Joshua finally led his eager troops to the walls of Jericho they discovered there was more waiting to be done – fortunately not as painful as the time at Gilgal! This was to be no ordinary battle. Siege towers, scaling ladders, catapults and battering rams were forgotten. Swords and spears were laid aside; all the soldiers had to do was to march around the walls. We all know the story well; it's one of the most famous in the Bible. However, it's worth asking just five important questions to learn the lessons of waiting at Jericho.

1. How did Joshua know what to do? The answer is PRAYER. History shows us that Joshua was a first-rate strategist and army general. He was wise and experienced. But no battle manual would have told him to march his army thirteen times around a hostile city over seven days without firing a single arrow! Joshua's unique defeat of Jericho had nothing to do with his luck or his experience. Joshua had a relationship with God and he maintained that relationship by constant contact. Joshua knew what to do because God told him what to do and, no matter how strange, Joshua did it.

2. How many times did the people march around Jericho? Read Joshua 6 and you'll find it was thirteen times. I've a strong suspicion that if they'd marched twelve times or fourteen times or even a hundred times round they would not have achieved the same result. It wasn't that thirteen was a lucky or magic number. It was simply that God had told them to do it that way and they did. The answer is OBEDIENCE.

3. How long did it take? Again the answer is in the book. Seven days! I'm sure that by the time they got to the third day people would already be scratching their heads and wondering. Thirteen circuits of the wall in a week must have been tiring and frustrating. Why couldn't they just get on with it? Waiting can be boring and repetitive. We wonder if we are ever going to get what we are waiting for. The answer is PERSEVERANCE. Being willing to wait, despite the discomfort, doubt and disbelief, always attracts the favour of God.

4. What can we learn from this most famous biblical battle? The answer is SPIRITUAL WARFARE. Here is a picture of how we are to fight. It is to be through prayer, in obedience, and by perseverance. Our fight is not against flesh and blood (Ephesians 6:12). We are called to a supernatural conflict and we only have *one enemy*. As a vicar and as a clown I long for people to just trust Jesus and not do the work of the devil. The trouble is, we forget this simple fact and, by thought word and deed, we start knocking seven bells out of one another! We are never encouraged to fight other people but always to direct our warfare against satan.

5. Finally – how many people shouted on the last day? All of them! The answer is UNITY. I can't help wondering that if just one or two in that vast crowd had remained silent would the walls still have come down? What I do know is that there is very little we can achieve without doing it together. When I think of all those people outside Jericho, from babes in arms to old grannies on sticks, shouting for all they're worth, it gives me a lovely picture of the Church. It's like the 'Yes!' we shout when we get the long-awaited exam result, or the huge sigh we let out when the tannoy says: 'Mr Guest? The doctor will see you now.' At last, the waiting is over and we can go in.

But it's the waiting that's important.

God, the Eternal Father, wants his children to Sabbath. He wants us to rest, to await his will and purpose as he prepares us for what is to come. He wants us to depend on him, to know beyond doubt that this is his victory.

As Joshua stood near Jericho, contemplating the battle that lay ahead, we read that he was approached by a man with a drawn sword (Joshua 5:13). Joshua challenged him. 'Who goes there? Friend or foe?' The man answers that he is neither but that he has come as the commander of the Lord's army. He is saying in effect: 'I've not come to take sides. I've come to take over!' God is in charge from the beginning and he knows what he is doing. Joshua is commanded to remove his shoes even as Moses was, forty years before. The place Joshua stands upon is holy for he is doing a holy thing and this is a holy meeting. He is meeting with the Lord!

Many hundreds of years later, twelve confused disciples waited for a meal. Unlike Joshua, they were unaware that they were about to face a battle, but they must have been equally anxious. They didn't know it, but the place whereon they stood was also holy ground. A man without a sword met them there and asked them to remove their shoes.

And then he washed their feet.

17

FIFTH BREATH:
WAITING IN WEAKNESS

In 1981, when I was an assistant minister in a
Midlands mining town, I contracted an acute dose
of glandular fever, coupled with hepatitis. It is
unusual for me to be ill but on this occasion I was
off work for six weeks and lost a stone and a half in
weight. After this experience I periodically found
myself suffering recurrences of the fatigue I'd felt
during the illness. Occasionally, I would become
very disorientated and confused. My doctor put it
down to the pressures of work and I was pre-
scribed the usual pick-me-ups.

My bouts of tiredness were never enough to
seriously affect my work but in 1986 (now living in
Liverpool) I was concerned enough to visit my
doctor again and, following hospital tests, was
diagnosed with PVFS: Post Viral Fatigue
Syndrome. In those days such conditions were
often disparagingly referred to as 'Yuppie Flu',
since it seemed to be a problem affecting young
business people and was thought to be largely psy-
chosomatic. (I must say, this was probably the first
and only time I have been associated with the
'young and upwardly mobile'. Nowadays I tend to
feel neither!)

As the years passed and we moved down south to Essex, my condition improved and I seemed virtually free of it. However, in 1995, following a minor post-operative infection, the illness returned with a vengeance. I often found myself struggling with fatigue and in addition I now had aching pains in my arms, legs, shoulders and back. My condition, I discovered, was Myalgic Encephalomyelitis, also known as Chronic Fatigue Syndrome. In one of those peculiar 'coincidences' that can only come from God, it was around this time that Kim was made redundant from her job in London and went to work for the ME Association, based, of all places, in my home parish of Stanford-le-Hope!

Myalgic Encephalomyelitis

According to the ME Association ME is a physical illness characterised by exhaustion and overwhelming fatigue, muscle weakness, pain, mood changes and flu-like feelings. These symptoms tend to fluctuate from hour to hour and day to day, and are often made worse by physical and mental overactivity. There are several charities associated with the condition and a number of resources available to deal with it. Some of these are listed at the end of this book.

At the time of writing I am visiting various specialists and trying different treatments for my condition. I thank God that I am still able to be a vicar and a clown as well as an ME sufferer and that I am still able to smile. Most people Kim and I come into contact with, who have the condition, are far worse than I am. Some are wheelchair bound, many spend a great deal of time in bed and there is a lot of sadness and despair associated with the problem. One enormous difficulty is that ME is still so little understood and those who have it are sometimes thought of as malingerers or hypochondriacs. It's bad enough to suffer pain, exhaustion and frustration without other people thinking you're putting it on!

Another problem is in the diagnosis of ME where there is some divergence of opinion in the medical profession. The condition may be wholly viral, as some think, or it may be psychological. It may be stress related or there may be a connection with chemicals in the atmosphere or a variety of environmental factors.

Most people learn to cope with the illness (and 'cope' is, of course, a relative word) and some people recover from it. I have also met people who have been healed of it. Liz Babbs, author of *Can God Help ME?*, which includes her story of healing,[1] is a member of the Christian Dance Fellowship. She demonstrates in a very moving dance, her progression through the condition of ME to her eventual healing.

Praying for Healing

I have been frequently prayed for but so far have not been healed. I believe very much in divine healing and have seen people healed by God from different ailments on a number of occasions. My present condition also gives me some small understanding of those who have been prayed for and whose state appears unchanged.

To all who are reading this I would want to say that my condition is peculiar to me: the lessons I have learned apply to me and may not apply to others. Some who have the same condition as me are in a far worse state. Others may have varying kinds of disability that affect them physically, mentally or emotionally. Neverthe-less, I hope some of the foolish thoughts I have regarding my weakness may speak to you. Perhaps the most foolish of all is that I am glad I have had ME and that I thank God for it. There are things that I have learned through the pain, tiredness and frustration that I could not have learned anywhere else.

If you have ME or indeed, any other debilitating illness, you might think of the previous paragraph as being almost heresy. Please don't misunderstand me. I don't welcome my condition. There are times when it drives my family up the wall and I often feel I've let down those who pray so faithfully for me without seeing a result. I'd gladly put the whole illness in a bag and drop it down a well if I could. Liz Babbs writes of those who refer to ME as 'a living hell'. But God is very gracious. I'm still working (quite hard actually) and I'm still clowning. Sometimes, God even gives me the strength to dance and even ride rollercoasters (see Chapter 12!). And waiting in weakness has revealed to me some very profound things about my relationship with God.

There are days when it would be so much easier to stay in bed or give in to the fatigue and just go to sleep. I find myself working out what I need to do upstairs so I don't have to make too many painful trips. Stairs and hills can be a real strain on the legs and standing for extended periods can cause further trauma for the back. Strangely enough, the illness is not consistent. Some days I can walk and bend and even cope with quite steep flights of stairs with very little pain. On others it can be a real effort to do the simplest things. Exercise is almost impossible on a regular basis so I am very unfit. The squash and weight training I used to do has had to be set aside for now. The other frustration is memory. They tell me there are four signs of ME I know that the first is losing your memory but I can't recall the other two (or was it three?). Actually, my memory has become terribly erratic. I can remember poems and lists of information but I've forgotten whole chunks of my childhood or what I did last week. My family gets very frustrated when I keep repeating things. My family gets very frustrated when I keep repeating things. My family gets very frustrated when I keep repeating things.

God's Most Intimate Touch

I'm very pleased to say that through it all the one thing that has not deserted me (most of the time!) is my weird sense of humour and the hope that one day I will be better. If you're reading this as an ME sufferer, or you have a similar condition, I would never dream of sermonising or lecturing you. Doubtless you will have different experiences to me. One thing I do know is that we must never lose hope. Janet Hurrell, herself an ME sufferer, writes in *A Helping Hand through M.E.*:

> For me, the key factors to improvement are rest, diet, supplements, relaxation, freedom from stress (including peace and quiet!) and a positive mental attitude. Above all, don't ever give up hope.[2]

Hal Lindsey says, 'man can live about forty days without food, about three days without water, about eight minutes without air but only one second without hope'.[3] Hope really is one of the greatest factors to enable sufferers from Chronic Fatigue to keep going. As we wait, we hope. I should know; I've been living in hope for some years!

Despite the fear and trauma associated with long-term disability there are many benefits available for those who wait in weakness. I don't know many clowns with CFS but I do know of many disabled people who give wonderfully of themselves through the media of the creative arts. The group I belong to, Full Circle, has a number of very fine performers in a variety of disciplines.

Having an ongoing medical condition can focus the spirit wonderfully. I felt very humbled to hear Joni Eareckson Tada speak to a group of us some years ago. Joni was rendered virtually quadriplegic in a diving accident many years before and despite numerous operations and much prayer has remained almost completely paralysed from the neck down. As she speaks from her wheelchair Joni is a very attractive lady with a glowing and beautiful spirit. She explained to us that lying on her back unable to move she was forced to look up into the face of God and realise she was totally in his hands. Joni has discovered the secret of suffering and the way God can lovingly transfigure us through pain and disability. Suffering is what some writers have called '*God's most intimate touch*'. In his first letter the apostle Peter wrote:

> Dear friends, do not be surprised at the painful trial you are suffering, as though something

strange were happening to you. But rejoice that
you participate in the sufferings of Christ, so
that you may be overjoyed when his glory is
revealed.

(1 Peter 4:12, 13)

Peter knew what it was to suffer both pain and persecution and the church to which he wrote in Asia
Minor was experiencing the same. Peter had
known Jesus face to face but he also knew Jesus
wouldn't always simply heal a condition or
remove an obstacle. Often the Lord would just
walk with him through it. Bob Gass says that if the
Lord doesn't deliver you, he'll defend you and if he
doesn't defend you, he'll develop you. But whatever happens, Jesus has promised to be with us and
never, never to forsake us!

The secret to dealing with pain and persecution,
heartache and suffering is to offer it to God. Like
Jerry, in the earlier chapter, we have two choices.
We can get bitter or we can get better. But we do
have to be prepared to wait. My own experience is
that God always answers my prayers but not
always in the way I expect. I can pray: 'Lord, please
heal my ME!' or 'Father, I need your grace to get
me through today. Keep me from selfish self-pity.
Help me to make a difference!' I can pray all sorts
of prayers for myself and for others. Sometimes
God says 'Yes', sometimes he says 'No', but most
times he says: 'Wait!'

Waiting on God

Waiting *for* God can also be seen in terms of waiting *on* God. Having been a silver-service waiter in
a small hotel in Hove I know what it is to be at the
beck and call of others. Sometimes, being a vicar

feels a little the same! The white collar I usually wear around my neck is certainly not a displaced halo. It is a badge of ownership and just as a dog collar on a dog shows it belongs to someone, so my dog collar shows I belong to someone too. Being a waiter for God reminds me that I have been called to serve him and to do his will and that means being prepared to wait to see what he wants. In Luke 17 Jesus reminds his disciples that it is the job of the servant to wait on his master before he takes any care of his own needs and afterwards to say: 'We are unworthy servants; we have only done our duty' (Luke 17:10). What a joy to know that the one who calls us 'servants' also calls us 'friends'!

One of the most frustrating forms of waiting is during illness or enforced convalescence. When we've taken our health and mobility for granted and been used to managing the daily routines of life unaided it can be a devastating shock to have this taken away and to be suddenly dependent upon the whims of others. To lose the use of one's legs and arms or to find sight or hearing suddenly impaired or to discover that the mind is no longer capable of formulating reasonable and cogent thought: these are the kinds of scenarios where waiting is most hard. These are not alien things of course, for most of us will one day grow old and steadily lose the precious gift of choice. Waiting in a bed or in a hospital or in a home can be an empty kind of waiting. Many of my older friends tell me this kind of enforced waiting can be desperately irksome and meaningless. Waiting in weakness can be even harder when there is no certainty of resolution or healing. Even this is not irredeemable.

Waiting for God

God always hears us and God is always near us. And his grace will never fail us. As we wait, in sickness or in health, we have a promise of a future home prepared for those who wait. The writer to the Hebrews says:

> There remains, then, a Sabbath-rest for the people of God; for anyone who enters God's rest also rests from his own work, just as God did from his. Let us, therefore, make every effort to enter that rest . . .
>
> (Hebrews 4:9–11)

In *The Lord of the Rings* by J.R.R. Tolkien, Frodo the Hobbit, seared by the memory of the terrible One Ring and wounded by tooth, knife and sting, desperately seeks comfort, despite having passed through the ordeals of his quest. 'Where shall I find rest?' he cries. His rest is finally found in the lands to the West, beyond the Sundering Seas: a picture of heaven. For us there is a rest for now and a rest to come, and both involve waiting. And although the waiting may at times be unpleasant, we will find God there, waiting with us.

All through the pages of the Bible we will find the stories of people who waited. Noah was 500 years in a world steeped in wickedness before God spoke to him. Abraham and Sarah waited most of their married life before receiving a son in their dotage. Joseph languished for years in Pharaoh's jail before God 'remembered' him. Moses was forty years in Egypt and forty years with sheep and goats before God called him into ministry. Joshua waited before Jericho; timid Gideon and mighty

Samson both waited. Naomi waited in her bitter bereavement and God rewarded her. Saul refused to wait and tragically lost his kingdom. David waited faithfully during the many years between his anointing by Samuel and his final coronation. Elijah had to wait before God's still voice commissioned him. Jeremiah waited without seeing in his lifetime the fulfilment of his prophecies. Esther waited before the king (twelve months of beauty treatments in his harem!) and her faithful stepfather Mordecai likewise. Nehemiah also waited before the king and Daniel waited in prayer seventy years in Babylon. Jonah was obliged to wait three days in a very unusual place and it was there, in the belly of a great fish, he was finally obedient to God's will. Zechariah waited to receive his voice and his son, and Elizabeth and Mary waited for the awesome promise of God to be manifest. Simeon and Anna, those two incredible old people, waited decades in the temple until God should reveal to them his Messiah. In obedience to the Lord's command the disciples waited in Jerusalem until they should receive 'the power from on high'. Paul waited to go to Rome and later, as he waited in prison, he wrote his letters. John waited until he was a very old man to receive the revelation that now comprises the last book of the Bible.

But the greatest waiter of all is God himself! Through eternity he waited until he should reveal himself and take flesh and walk the earth. Earnestly now he waits to hear our prayers and looks to see the day when all his own shall be gathered for the wedding banquet of his Son. God waits more patiently than anyone; for he is gracious and longsuffering, slow to anger and abounding in love and truth. Since God is so 'longsuffering', he knows what it is to suffer as we wait and the benefits and blessings that waiting brings.

I am not a good waiter. Even in weakness and disability I chafe to get going, to see the job done, to finish the tasks for the day. I'm impatient and slow to change and wait and be still and listen to God. I'm not good at waiting but I'm learning. And God hasn't finished with me yet. Perhaps that's why ME has taken me and forced me to wait and to learn and to be still.

When I was growing up in the late sixties I often used to go with my grandfather to stay with his sister in Forest Row, Sussex. I can still remember those mouth-watering apple pies and rich fruit-cakes she used to bake! In those days my grandfather liked to walk and we would take strolls across the Ashdown Forest. Together we'd walk to the little hamlet of Coleman's Hatch and, at the little tavern there my grandfather would get half a pint of mild, and bring me out a glass of lemonade. Lunch was always 1.00 pm sharp at my great-aunt's and so grandfather would walk up the lane to catch the bus back home.

But I would run back across the forest.

In my mind's eye I see that boy now, running like the wind, leaping across the streams and clumps of bracken, making nothing of the hills and dips, racing the bus to be home first, running for the sheer joy of being young and alive.

I know that one day God will heal my ME I know that one day I shall run again and not be weary. And on that day, Jesus will run with me.

but those who wait for the LORD shall
   renew their strength.
   they shall mount up on wings like eagles;
they shall run and not be weary,
   they shall walk and not faint.

(Isaiah 40:31 NRSV)

18

SIXTH BREATH:
DO LESS – BE MORE

The famous 'Gorilla Joke' has being doing the rounds of churches and conferences for some years now and is a really effective tool for illustrating the stark realities of life and ministry. I don't know that any single person can claim the credit for originating the story but I first heard it told at a day conference in St Helen's by my good friend John Leach. Just in case you haven't heard it . . .

An unemployed man is leafing through the situations vacant when he sees an ad requesting help at his local zoo. He applies for the job and gets an interview. His prospective employer is very pleased with his appearance and manner and delighted with his CV and references. After a short conversation the man is offered the job. He readily accepts but is interested to know what the position actually requires. The interviewer is somewhat embarrassed to explain that theirs is only a small zoo with few resources. Last month, their star attraction, Samson the Gorilla, suddenly died and they were unable to afford to replace him. The man's job would be to dress up as a gorilla, take Samson's place, and entertain the visitors! Our hero is taken somewhat aback but is reassured he will receive complete training in a special Primate Impersonators Induction Course. A week later finds the man, impressively disguised in a most lifelike gorilla suit, pacing up and down the ape enclosure, wowing the crowds. He actually develops a little routine. He runs along a tree branch, waving his long arms and blowing raspberries for all he's worth, slides down the rope ladder, rushes across the floor, leaps onto the rubber tyre, swings wildly across the cage and crashes into the wire mesh, making loud gorilla noises.

This seems to go down very well with the punters and the crowds grow. The man gains in confidence and his routine grows even more impressive as the weeks go by. One day he is visited by the local sixth form girls' biology class and he is determined to really impress them. He shoots along his branch, down the rope and across the floor of the cage at breakneck speed. Unfortunately, he steps on a discarded banana skin, careers across the floor, misses the tyre completely and crashes into the side wall of the cage. He smashes through the wall into the next enclosure and, moments later, finds himself gazing up into the slavering jaws of an enormous black-maned lion! At this point, the man totally loses it, forgets his role and purpose and yells at the top of his voice, 'Someone get me out of here!' The lion looks down at him and hisses: 'Shut up, you fool, or we'll both be out of a job!'

Gorilla Suits

The point the story illustrates is that we all reach points in our lives when we are suddenly overwhelmed by our circumstances. Up to that point we've been coasting merrily along, wearing all the

ight costumes and masks and impressing those
around us quite effectively. We go through the
ight routines, at work, at home, in church, on the
golf course, with our friends. We even begin to feel
pleased with ourselves that everyone has been
aken in by our performance. No one fully knows
he scared little person behind the mask: the man in
he gorilla suit. Then one day something happens.
t may be a major crisis like sudden illness or
bereavement. It may be a relatively minor incident:
he straw that breaks the camel's back. The
esponse we make, like the man gazing up at the
ion, is to yell: 'Someone get me out of here!' How
many times have we at least thought: 'Stop the
world, I want to get off'?

What we discover when we find ourselves
screaming with fear, realising we've been exposed
or what we really are, is that everyone else is in the
ame position as us. The smiling, coping, compe-
ent people we envied, the ones who'd 'got it all
ogether', were also dressed in costumes and wear-
ng masks. They are just as fearful at being found
put as we are. Doesn't that tell us something very
profound about the human condition?

As we work, we often do so fearful that we will
be exposed for what we really are: small minded
and selfish. We try to impress yet doubt our ability
o succeed. Our 'play' consists of competitive urges
hat really say we want to be top, even at the
expense of others. Masks and makeup produce a
estless fear that allows us little opportunity to be
purselves or to show those around us what we are
eally like. And always present is the constant fear
of being found out. We are fearful that it is only us
who are like this and yet almost everyone we meet

is hiding behind a façade.

The Scripture Union video *In the Bin* shows a very similar world where everyone wears masks. Jesus is portrayed as a barefaced dustbinman who removes people's masks and throws them in the dustbin. In the end they murder the dustbinman, and only then do they perceive the truth he came to bring them. Jesus encourages us to remove our masks and step out of the costumes we wear and to face up to reality. He already knows our weaknesses and fears and he wants to set us truly free.

> And we, who with unveiled faces all reflect the Lord's glory, are being transformed into his likeness with ever-increasing glory, which comes from the Lord, who is the Spirit.
>
> (2 Corinthians 3:18)

Society at the beginning of this new millennium is very happy with its masks and costumes provided that they are never seen as such. This civilised masquerade is virtual reality but never reality itself. It is clever and sophisticated and, like the special effects of the great blockbusters, we can almost believe it is real. But it isn't. Inside the gorilla suit is a man, *almost* believing he's a gorilla, but knowing deep inside that he's just as human as the people peering through the bars.

Perhaps it takes the fear of being eaten alive to jolt us out of our virtual realities to the truth around us. Maybe it is the sufferings of life that enable us to remember who we really are and not just what we are supposed to do. Work may authenticate us and play may entertain us but it is when we rest and wait that we begin to perceive the true person behind the mask.

You might think it a bit rich for a Whiteface clown who wears a multicoloured jumpsuit to be presuming to lecture on masks and makeup. Or even worse, for a vicar who dresses up in a variety of old-fashioned robes on a Sunday, to complain about costumes. That's as maybe, but at least that make-up and those robes are real. It's the virtual ones we need to fear. The 'I'm OK' face, the 'sincerely concerned' face, the 'Jack the lad' look and the 'cool, calm and collected' expression. Our masks are designed to impress and to make others think well of us. They are expressions of what we do but not of who we are. You don't have to be a clown to understand this, but if you are it helps!

Make a Space and Hold On

They say hard work never hurt anyone. Actually it did – it hurt lots of people. People who forgot how to play or were too busy to rest. People like you and me. The cult science fiction series *Babylon 5* is not usually thought of as imparting theological truth, but in the last episode of Series 4 they drew attention to the biblical word 'Selah'. This strange word occurs only in the book of Psalms (sixty-nine times) and in the book of Habakkuk (three times). Nowhere else. This peculiar literary or musical term is thought by some to mean simply 'pause'. It is an encouragement to stop and wait, to rest and evaluate. To quietly look and see what happens.

Pausing to rest between bouts of work can make a lot of difference. It can even improve the work. When we are exhausted by meaningless labour or depressed from lack of purpose, true rest for the soul can put back the shape and focus in our lives.

Jesus said:

> 'Come to me, all you who are weary and bur-
> dened, and I will give you rest. Take my yoke
> upon you and learn from me, for I am gentle
> and humble in heart, and you will find rest for
> your souls.'
>
>   (Matthew 11:28, 29)

Blowing up a balloon is hard work. If you forget
the space at the nipple end, or neglect to let out a
little bit of pressure at the nozzle end, you could be
in trouble. Worse: if you forget to tie the knot or let
go and lose it completely then you will lose all
shape and direction. Remember, it's what's inside
that counts!

They tell me the husky dogs of the frozen North
are classic ergomaniacs. From dawn to dusk they
pull the sledges across the snow and ice, desperate
to be moving on and doing their jobs. Bred for
work it seems they can do little else. For huskies
never retire. When they decide it's time to stop
work they just lay down and die and their masters
find them in the morning, stiff in the snow.

But we are not huskies.

A while ago I stood up at a meeting of church
leaders because I felt guilty. I find so much of what
we do is motivated by guilt. The extra toys for the
children, the phone call home, the flowers for the
wife, that extra hug; these can all be expressions of
guilt. On this occasion my guilt was prompted by a
powerful sermon on reaching out to the
unchurched. I knew that I didn't spend enough
time telling other people the good news about
Jesus. I knew I had the gifts of an evangelist but I

wasn't spending nearly enough time doing the ministry. I wasn't visiting members of my own congregation as frequently as I should. I just wasn't doing enough!

I strode up to the front and stood among a crowd of others being prayed for by the leaders of the church. My hands were gripped together tightly and my face screwed up in the intensity of my desire to do God's will. I asked God to forgive me for not working hard enough. I prayed that he would fill me with an even greater fervency to serve him and reach others. Then I prepared myself to be overwhelmed with the power of God!

All at once I became aware of God smiling at me much as a father smiles at a son who breathlessly tells him: 'I've washed the car, I've mowed the lawn, I've done all my homework – now what do you want me to do Dad?' God the Father smiled at me and in that moment I felt peace wash over me like a refreshing shower. All my fervour and intensity drained away and I was content to just be in the presence of my Lord. I smiled back.

'Relax, John,' he said to me. 'Do less. Be more.'

So simple. So profound. All my struggling to please and to impress: all my 'gorilla posturing' counted for very little in the eternal scheme of things. The Father didn't love me for what I could do for him. He loves me for who I am! How easily I could wear the mask of the evangelist, the pastor or the teacher but in effect all I was doing was saying: 'Look at me! See how busy I am. Be impressed!'

As I stood there pondering these things and basking in the unconditional acceptance of God, I overheard the preacher asking one of his team to take over as he was late for a meeting. 'Good heavens!' I thought to myself. 'He's just like me after all!' I smiled up at God again and returned to my seat a better man.

> As Jesus and his disciples were on their way, he came to a village where a woman named Martha opened her home to him. She had a sister called Mary, who sat at the Lord's feet listening to what he said. But Martha was distracted by all the preparations that had to be made. She came to him and asked, 'Lord, don't you care that my sister has left me to do the work by myself? Tell her to help me!'
>
> 'Martha, Martha,' the Lord answered, 'you are worried and upset about many things, but only one thing is needed. Mary has chosen what is better, and it will not be taken away from her.'
>
> (Luke 10:38–42)

We might be forgiven for thinking that preparations 'have to' be made, particularly ones as important as housework and cooking. We might be excused for assuming that work has to be done. But Jesus' gentle rebuke to Martha puts it all into startling perspective. 'Mary has chosen what is better . . .'

He could even have said: 'Do less. Be more.'

CONCLUSION:
PROPHETIC BALLOON
MODELLING

Well, we made it: the end of the book! We've shared some foolish thoughts on Work, Rest and Play and hopefully we've learned something. I've learned that even clowns can write books and you've learned that you can get through a book with a title as ridiculous as 'Prophetic Balloon Modelling'. Together we've explored something of the balance and focus of life and tried to discover the significance of work, rest and play. How did you get on with making the balloon dove, by the way? Who did you give it to? What happened?

I hope you remembered to leave that little space at the end and that you let a bit of air out before you tied off. In balloon modelling, as in life, these things are vital! I don't know whether balloons have helped you to think a bit more about balance and focus but hopefully we've both learned a little more about work, rest and play. If nothing else, I hope I've made you smile!

Work is Good

Work is good because we all need something to do. However, we've seen how easy it is for work to get out of hand and begin to take over. If we're not careful it can turn into a many-headed monster and make us its slave. Whether we're employed, self-employed, unemployed or a vicar, we need to be careful about allowing what we do (or don't do!) to authenticate us. We are a great deal more than a job.

Work is always best when it is purpose-led rather than activity-driven. Having a clear aim, short, middle and long term, can be a big help. Remember: if you aim at nothing, you are sure to hit it! Choice is a precious thing in the sphere of work but it can feel like a pressure if we allow ourselves to be overwhelmed by minor decisions. Passion can quickly become drained by choice overload, meaningless activity and busyness. Focussing on Safe Places, Still Times and Special Friends can restore this. Enthusiasm combats cynicism and helps to overcome discouragement.

Work is good in its place but it should be kept in its place. Six-sevenths of our time may be available in which to work but not all of it. An eight-hour workday may be an old-fashioned idea but it's a good yardstick. A good job, well done, can provide enormous satisfaction but many jobs are just activities endured in order to earn money. If work becomes an end in itself then it loses purpose and our balance has gone. It is probably true that we 'have to' work, but work is not the whole of our lives.

Play is Better

Play is better because we like to play. Play teaches us life skills in an enjoyable context. We discover the value of relationship and the pleasure that comes from laughter. We begin to appreciate the power of forgiveness and how to resolve disagreement and conflict. The ups and downs of the rollercoaster of life are put into proper perspective.

Play helps us to relate our story, to listen to the stories of others and to appreciate the great stories of life. The games we play as children and as adults shape our personalities. The dynamic interplay of vulnerability and encouragement releases us to be the people we were supposed to be. Potentials begin to be realised.

Play is better because it reminds us that we were children and, deep inside, we are children still. And Jesus told us that the kingdom of God would belong to such as these. If work reminds us that we belong to a community, then play shows we belong to a family.

Rest is Best

Rest is best! Rest provides the balance to work and play. It is the diastole in the rhythm of life. Rest is a holy time, designed by God and modelled by him for our benefit. Through it we learn to review and revere, to observe and attach value to. We discover the importance of renouncing purposeless activity and embracing relaxation. We remember that we were slaves but now we can choose to be free!

Resting helps us to wait for God. We endeavour to learn patience as we wait, in need or in plenty, in sorrow or in joy. At the traffic lights of life we seek to discover the colour ahead of us, whether we are to wait, get ready or go. We may perceive that the God for whom we wait also waits for us. In the stillness we discover his unconditional love for us.

Above all, rest is best because it shows us how to do less and to be more. If work reminds us we belong to a community and play shows we belong to a family, then rest helps us realise that, ultimately, we belong to God.

Focus and Balance

In the swirling, rushing, sorrowful, foolish business of life, Work, Rest and Play are what we need to give us focus and balance. If we were children it would be like riding a bike; if we were clowns it would be like juggling or walking the slackrope. We climb on and struggle to meet the challenge of finding the right balance. Children and clowns tend to fall off frequently (well, clowns anyway) before they begin to master the constantly shifting technique of balance. But falling off is all part of the fun and pain of living.

In the last chapter of his book *The Shape of Living*, Professor David Ford uses, instead of balance, the concept of dance to describe the interplay and interweaving of life. The Greek term *perichoresi*, he says, was used by the early church to describe what took place within the life of God.[1] I would want to suggest that we, made in the image of God, participate in a similar kind of dance as we foolishly move to balance Work, Rest and Play. The three experiences can be like a dancing partner: coy and innocent, intimate and close, wild and invigorating, yet constantly moving, romancing us into the dance of life.

But, what do I know about it? These are foolish thoughts. I am not a theologian; I'm a clown! I have to work, I like to play and I need to rest. I'm also a disciple, which means I'm still learning. God isn't done with me yet and I've not finished living. As a vicar and as a clown I believe fervently in God but what's more important: he believes in me! Work, Rest and Play are what he's given me to make sense of who I am and to accompany me on the journey to what he wants me to be.

One Thing Only

The Bible tells me that only 'one thing' is essential.
It tells me this three times. In Philippians 3 verse
13, it is something I do, as in a meaningful task.
Like Paul, I fix my eyes on the goal ahead and press
forward. In Psalm 27 verse 4, it is something I ask,
as a child might ask his father for something special. Like David, I need to seek the Lord in his
house and gaze upon his beauty, for that is my
playground and my temple. And in Luke 10 verse
42, it is something I need neither do nor ask but just
be. Like Mary, I choose what is better: to rest at the
feet of Jesus. This one thing I do, one thing I ask,
this one thing only I need. In work, in play and in
rest: just one thing.

Clowning and Dancing

So . . . why 'Prophetic Balloon Modelling'? What's
the third reason for the title? Yes, it is a bit foolish:
just what a clown would choose, and it may possibly attract the kind of people who like a book with
'prophetic' in the title, but what's that got to do
with work, rest and play? First of all, let me tell you
a story. Strangely enough, it has to do with dancing.

In 1995 I was asked to speak at the national conference of the Christian Dance Fellowship of
Britain and to lead some clown workshops. I readily agreed (I love preaching and leading workshops!) but I was intrigued as to what dancers
would want with clowns. I was also a bit nervous
about mixing it with lissom athletic types, prancing
around in leotards. After all, I am a *little* tubby. I
needn't have worried; some of them were lissom
and athletic but some of them were my size as well.

And the nicest bunch of Christian ladies (and men) you could wish to meet.

I had quite a full programme to manage. In addition to five workshops and Bible studies I also had some afternoon seminars to lead. I decided to do one on story telling and one on balloon modelling. When they asked me what I would be calling the latter I said, off the top of my head, 'Prophetic Balloon Modelling'. Now, there isn't very much on the top of my head so I wondered where the phrase came from. By that time I'd been including balloon modelling in my clowning for about three years. I could do all the usual things: dog, mouse, lion, swan, flower, single span suspension bridge. It was great fun but was there really anything prophetic about it? I suppose that may depend on your understanding of the word 'prophetic'.

Defining the Prophetic

The *Concise Oxford Dictionary* defines a prophet as a 'revealer or interpreter of God's will'. If someone or something is 'prophetic', then, it will disclose the purposes and nature of God and his kingdom. Some of the prophets in the Bible were very weird characters. I don't recall any of them working with balloons but they did get up to some other activities that were equally strange. Jeremiah had to wear a belt, hide it and then dig it up again. Jonah got eaten by a fish and then had to sit under a vine tree. Hosea had to marry a prostitute. Agabus had to tie up the apostle Paul hand and foot. And as for poor Ezekiel – you won't believe what he had to do! (You can read about it in Ezekiel chapters 3 to 5.) Prophecy is not always strange but it is often foolish. God in his foolish wisdom will offend the

mind to reveal the heart. Clowns really are messengers of God and sometimes they are prophets as
well, for their foolishness will touch the heart in
ways that ordinary words cannot. You don't have
to be a clown to understand this, but if you are it
helps!

Balloon Messages

As I began to prepare for my seminar, still wondering why I'd had the notion to call it *prophetic* balloon modelling, God spoke to me. What he said to
me made me laugh and then it made me think and
then it made me cry. The balloon modelling *was*
prophetic and the activity I was engaged in *was* a
foolish demonstration of the nature of God and the
message of the gospel.

There's nothing particularly special about balloon material. Modelling balloons are somewhat
different to your average run-of-the-mill party balloons, and you buy them in bulk from a special
supplier, but they're essentially the same things.
They are made from pure natural biodegradable
latex and, deflated, they're not much to look at, a
bit foolish really. But then I think about all the
insignificant foolish things that God uses to reveal
his purposes. I think about Balaam's donkey and
Gideon's bagel and I remember the kid who killed
a giant and the prophet who lost his temper with a
worm. I recall what Jesus did with 180 gallons of
washing up water and how he used a small boy's
packed lunch.

But God chose the foolish things of the world to
shame the wise; God chose the weak things of
the world to shame the strong. He chose the

lowly things of this world and the despised things – and the things that are not – to nullify the things that are, so that no-one may boast before him.

(1 Corinthians 1:27–29)

God takes ordinary things and makes them special. He takes ordinary people and makes them special too. Now things don't come much more foolish or weak or lowly or despised than a deflated balloon! And when it is shapeless and empty it is something that is not. God uses such things – so he told me.

Now there's a few things you need to know about balloons and balloon modelling. Balloons are often associated with parties, and with children and with celebration. There is a lot of interest and laughter when they are being stretched and inflated. Sometimes you lose your grip on them and they fly off, causing even more laughter. As you let the air out and then twist and shape them, they make all sorts of rude and peculiar noises, causing more laughter and some embarrassment. Very occasionally they burst (it only happens once, as I am quick to point out!), causing surprise and sometimes tears. You're recommended to blow modelling balloons up with a special pump (mine's called a 'Faster Blaster') but I generally prefer to inflate them with my own lungs. Harder, but more satisfying and, as you'll see in a moment, more prophetic!

When you inflate and model one or more balloons into a fantastical creation you invariably attract a crowd – adults as well as children. They are conversation pieces, crowd-pleasers. When you give one away, you've made a friend for life. I like to model them in unusual places: in restaurants and supermarkets, at serious board meetings and on trains and buses, even in churches. You'd be surprised at the amazing conversations that I have with people. Sometimes we even get round to talking about God.

Balloons, modelling and otherwise, evoke strange feelings in people. We take them home from parties and fast food outlets and leave them to go sad in a corner of the lounge. We see them sometimes high up in the girders of shopping centre ceilings or football stadiums and we love to carry them, jerking and bobbing merrily on brightly coloured ribbons. They lift our spirits and keep us looking up. And am I the only one who feels that funny poignant clutch at the heart, that sharp intake of breath, as I release one at a garden fete or show and watch it soaring, soaring up to the clouds? No – I'm not, in fact.

On August 27th, 1994, 1,592,744 balloons were released by Disney Home Video at Longleat House, Wiltshire. (Record from Guinness® World Records © Guinness World Records Ltd Guinness® is a Trade Mark of Guinness World Records Ltd.) Cheryl Baker, commentating for the BBC's *Recordbreakers*, was close to tears as she watched them soar into the sky.

Just like balloons, the kingdom of God is attractive. It is associated with children and with parties and celebration. It can bring laughter and tears and it is not unheard of for it to spring surprises. Balloons are certainly evocative and amazing. And there is yet something more prophetic about balloon modelling.

Breath of Life

When I inflate a balloon I give away the most precious part of myself. I give my own life's breath to fill that modelling balloon. When God first brought this to my attention it literally took my breath away! He does have a tendency to do that, you know. I think back to all the times that God has shown me something breathtaking. The vision he gave me on the day I was ordained. The lightning over the Grand Canyon and the majestic splendour of Niagara Falls. The wonder of holding my newly-born children in my arms. The sight of my lovely wife emerging from Los Angeles airport. And whenever he speaks to me and tells me something or shows me something, that, like inflating a modelling balloon, takes my breath away! And, did I not read somewhere, that to 'rest' is to 'take breath'?

And to give someone the gift of a balloon model containing a precious part of myself. A shaped piece of biodegradable latex – just a balloon – yet is containing the very breath from my own body.

Here is a picture of creation, of the God who makes something out of nothing and who then creates us in his own image. Here also is a picture of Jesus, who gives himself to us and for us, breathing out his last life's breath on the cross.

Here also is a picture of the Holy Spirit, the breath of God, intangible and invisible until he fills and inspires and gives shape to those he inhabits. Here also is a picture of the precious gospel of the Kingdom; a free gift to give away to any that will receive it and yet containing at its heart the priceless gift of life.

And all this in the foolishness of a balloon!

When God spoke to me so foolishly before that seminar I wondered if I'd heard him right. Could all this really be? And yet, on so many occasions since, I've seen the prophetic power of the balloon model at work, at rest and at play. In the wonder of children with balloon hats, in the laughter of friends with poodle dogs, in the wide-eyed growing comprehension of fellow travellers examining their latex flower, in the tears of an old lady as she cradles her beautiful white swan. To each the balloon speaks and reveals God. And above all I shall never forget the sight of Candy, professionally trained dancer and leader of the Christian Dance Fellowship, at the final conference session, dancing in worship, whirling and cavorting as she clutched her dove balloon model – symbol of the Holy Spirit. Holy ridiculous and wholly wonderful!

Foolish as it may seem, such dances and such balloons remind me of the vital focus of Work, Rest and Play, for such balances and such models show all three. As I seek to proclaim the kingdom of God in words and works and wonders, the balloon models speak to me. As Gof or John inflates them, intending for them to be used, I see the value of work, its purpose and its goal, and whether your work is open heart surgery, cooking school dinners, typing up reports or blowing up balloons, you too can make work have meaning. Meaninglessness is probably the major contributor to stress and breakdown in the field of work. True value comes when work has purpose and is a means to an end and never an end in itself.

As the balloon becomes a toy, a plaything for a child or a talking point for an adult, I see the value of play and whether your play is scrabble or football, jigsaws or line dancing, you too can have fun as you play. Attempting to invest play with meaning, to regard it in the same way as we should work, is to lose the point entirely. Play is intended to be 'meaningless' – for it is itself a goal and a destination. In the 'foolish play' of worship we discover the staggering truth that God likes us as we are and calls us to come and play with him, delighting in the wonder of his laughter and love. Ultimately, we discover this is not religion but relationship and that the greatest relationship of all is with him.

And when at last the balloon is still, lying silent upon the floor, I think of rest and the peace God intended we all should find in him. Or perhaps, in fancy, I might see that balloon released and, like my spirit, soar upward to heaven.

Ah, well . . . foolish reflections. You don't have to be a clown to understand them, but if you are . . .

NOTES

Chapter 1
1. Tim La Haye, *How to Manage Pressure Before Pressure Manages You* (Basingstoke: Marshall, Morgan & Scott (Marshalls), 1983).
2. David F. Ford, *The Shape of Living* (London: Harper-Collins (Fount), 1997).

Chapter 2
1. Reprinted from *Stress/Unstress* by Keith W. Sehnert (copyright 1981 Augsburg Publishing House, 1981, Minneapolis, MN). Used by permission of Augsburg Fortress. May not be reproduced further.
2. Rob Parsons, *The Sixty Minute Father* (London: Hodder & Stoughton, 1995).
3. Richard A. Swenson, MD, *Margin* (Colorado Springs, Colorado: NavPress). Used by permission of NavPress Publishing. All rights reserved. For copies of the book call 00-366-7788 1992.
4. Michio Kaku, *Visions* (Oxford: Oxford University Press, 1998).

Chapter 4
1. Richard A. Swenson, MD, *Margin*, op. cit.
2. David F. Ford, *The Shape of Living*, op. cit.
3. Frank Peretti, *Tilly* (Eastbourne: Monarch (Minstrel), 1989).

Chapter 5
1. Bob Gass, *The Word for Today* (Stoke-on-Trent: United Christian Broadcasters Ltd., 1998).

Chapter 6
1. Tony Campolo, *Carpe Diem* (Milton Keynes: Word Publishing, 1994).
2. Gordon MacDonald, *Restoring Your Spiritual Passion*

(Godalming: Highland Books, 1986).

3. Joseph Heller, quoted in *Restoring your Spiritual Passion*,
    Gordon MacDonald, op. cit.

4. *Wind Beneath my Wings. Words and music by* Larry Henley
    and Jeff Silbar © 1984 Warner House of Music and WB
    Gold Music Corp, USA. Warner/Chappell Music Ltd,
    London W6 8BS. Reproduced by permission of
    International Music Publications Ltd.

Chapter 7

1. Jean-Jacques Suurmond, *Word and Spirit at Play*,
    translated by John Bowden from the Dutch *Het Spel van
    Woord en Geest Uitgeverij Ten Have bv* (London: SCM, 1994).

2. Roly Bain, *Fools Rush In* (London: HarperCollins
    (Marshall Pickering), 1993).

3. Michael Frost, *Jesus the Fool* (Oxford: Lion (Albatross),
    1994).

4. Michael Card, © Birdwing Music/Mole End Music/EMI
    Christian Music Publishing/Copycare. PO Box 77,
    Hailsham; e.mail: music@copycare.com

5. Nicolai Poliakoff, *Coco the Clown* (London: Orion
    (J.M. Dent and Sons Ltd.), 1962).

Chapter 8

1. Max Lucado, *On the Anvil* (Wheaton, Illinois: Tyndale
    House Publishers Inc., 1985).

2. Tony Campolo, *The Kingdom of God is a Party* (Milton
    Keynes: Word Publishing, 1990).

Chapter 9

1. C.S. Lewis, *The Last Battle* (Harmondsworth: Penguin
    (Puffin), 1965).

Chapter 10

1. Eric Berne MD, *Games People Play* (Harmondsworth:
    Penguin, 1967).

2. John Gray, *Men are from Mars, Women are from Venus*
    (London: HarperCollins (Thorsons), 1993).

3. Ibid.
4. Rob Parsons, *The Sixty Minute Marriage* (London: Hodder & Stoughton, 1997).

Chapter 11

1. Walter Wangerin, *Ragman and Other Cries of Faith* (London: Hodder & Stoughton (Spire), 1993).
2. Jean-Jacques Suurmond, *Word and Spirit at Play*, op. cit.

Chapter 12

1. 1. Max Lucado, *On the Anvil,* op. cit.
2. Jean-Jacques Suurmond, *Word and Spirit at Play*, op. cit.
3. Ibid.

Chapter 13

1. Doris Longacre, *Living More with Less* (Scottdale, PA: Herald, 1980) quoted in Richard A. Swenson, *Margin,* op. cit.

Chapter 14

1. David F. Ford, *The Shape of Living,* op. cit.

Chapter 17

1. Elizabeth Babbs, *Can God Help ME?* (Guildford: Eagle, 1999).
2. Janet Hurrell, *A Helping Hand through M.E.* (Slough: Foulsham, 1998).
3. Hal Lindsey, *Hope for the Terminal Generation* (Old Tappan, NJ: Fleming H. Revell, 1976).

Chapter 19

1. David F. Ford, *The Shape of Living,* op. cit.
2. *The Guinness Book of Records,* 1996 edition, copyright 1995, Guinness Publishing Ltd. Guinness® is a Trade Mark of Guinness World Records Ltd.

Further Reading

Bain, Roly and Forbes, Patrick, *Clowning Glory* (London: National Society/Church House Publishing, 1995).

Brandon, Andrew, *Storytellers* (Milton Keynes: Scripture Union, 1994).

Duckworth, John, *Joan 'n' The Whale* (Eastbourne: Monarch (Minstrel), 1988).

Edwards, Gene, *A Tale of Three Kings* (Wheaton, Illinois: Tyndale House Publishers Inc., 1992).

Fynn, *Mister God This is Anna* (London: HarperCollins, 1974).

Gaukroger, Stephen and Mercer, Nick, *Frogs in Cream* (Milton Keynes: Scripture Union, 1990).

Frogs II, (Milton Keynes: Scripture Union, 1993).

Hercus, John, *David* (Leicester: Inter-Varsity Fellowship, 1967).

Jackson, Bob, *till The Fat Lady Sings* (Godalming: Highland, 1996).

Jacobs, Cindy, *Possessing the Gates of the Enemy* (London: HarperCollins (Marshall Pickering), 1991).

Manning, Brennan, *The Ragamuffin Gospel* (Stoke Mandeville: S.P. Trust (Alpha), 1995).

Marshall, Eric and Hample, Stuart, *Children's Letters to God* (London: HarperCollins, 1975).

Nouwen, Henri, *Clowning in Rome* (New York: Doubleday and Co. (Image), 1979).

In the Name of Jesus (London: Darton, Longman and Todd, 1989).

Plass, Adrian, *The Sacred Diary of Adrian Plass* (London: HarperCollins (Marshall Pickering), 1987).

Stress Family Robinson (London: HarperCollins (Marshall Pickering), 1995).

Broken Windows, Broken Lives (London: Hodder &

Stoughton, 1987).

Phillips, Bob, *Jest Another Good Clean Joke Book* (Eugene, Oregon: Harvest House, 1996).

Redpath, Alan, *Victorious Christian Living* (London: Pickering and Inglis Ltd., 1956).

Swindoll, Charles, *David* (Dallas, Texas: Word, 1997).

Tolkien, J.R.R., *The Lord of the Rings* (London: HarperCollins (Allen & Unwin), 1966).

Vanauken, Sheldon, *A Severe Mercy* (London: Hodder & Stoughton, 1977).

Wangerin, Walter, *The Book of the Dun Cow* (London: Hodder & Stoughton, 1990).

    The Book of Sorrows (London: Hodder & Stoughton, 1992).

    The Manger is Empty (London: Hodder (Spire), 1991).

Watts, Murray, *Rolling in the Aisles* (Crowborough: MARC/The Children's Society, 1987).

    Bats in the Belfry (Eastbourne: Monarch (Minstrel), 1989).

Yaconelli, Mike, *Yak Yak Yak!* (London: Harper-Collins (Marshall Pickering), 1991).

The Complete Works of William Shakespeare (London: Abbey Library, 1978).

Resources for ME/CFS

The two main organisations in this country are:

The ME Association
4 Corringham Road
Stanford-le-Hope
Essex
SS17 0EP
Office: 01375 642466; Information Line: 01375 361013 (1.30 pm–4.00 pm)
Listening Ear Service: 01375 361013 (after 4.00pm and at weekends)
01375 642466 (weekday afternoons)

and

Action for ME
PO Box 1302
Wells
Somerset
BA5 1YE
Office: 01749670799

The National ME Centre is based at:

Harold Wood Hospital
Romford
Essex
RM3 0BE
Office: 01708 378050

Other Resources

Full Circle Arts: Disability Arts Development
Agency
Greeheys Business Centre
10 Pencroft Way
Manchester
MU15 6JJ
0161 279 7878 (Fax: 0161 279 7879)
e.mail: user@full-circle-arts.demon.co.uk

The Happiness Project
Elms Court
Chapel Way
Botley
Oxford
OX2 9LP
01865 244414 (Fax: 01865 248825)

The WorkNet Partnership
56 Baldry Gardens
London
NW16 3DJ
0181 764 8080 (Fax: 0181 764 3030)
e.mail: training@worknetpartnership.org.uk
http://www.worknetpartnership.org.uk